——IDEALS OF——
THE SAMURAI
WRITINGS OF JAPANESE WARRIORS

Translation and Introduction
by
William Scott Wilson

Editor: Gregory N. Lee
Graphic Designer: Karen Massad

Cover
Calligraphy: J. Brems
Photography: Clinton Cleveland

Fourteenth printing 2000

OHARA **[Ⅲ]** PUBLICATIONS, INCORPORATED
SANTA CLARITA, CALIFORNIA

© 1982 Ohara Publications, Inc.
All rights reserved
Printed in the United States of America
Library of Congress Catalog Card Number: 82-60937
ISBN 0-89750-081-4

ACKNOWLEDGEMENTS

The translator and editor would like to express their thanks to the following for their kind permission to reprint the samurai portraits which appear in this volume:

The portrait of Asakura Toshikage on page 69 and the portrait of Hojo Soun on page 77 originally appeared in *Nihon no Shozo* (ed. National Museum of Kyoto, 1978); courtesy of Chuokoron-sha, Inc., publishers.

The portrait of Nabeshima Naoshige on page 116 originally appeared in *Dai Nihon Shiryo* (ed. Tokyo Daigaku Shiryo Hensanjo); the portraits of Kuroda Nagamasa on page 138 and Kato Kiyomasa on page 131 originally appeared in *Shozo senshu* (ed. Nihon Rekishi Gakkai, 1962); courtesy of Yoshikawa Kobunkan, publishers.

The portrait of Takeda Shingen on page 94 originally appeared in *Sekai Denki Daijiten, Vol. III* (1978); courtesy of The Rev. Naomichi Nakada of the Jorinji Monastery in Yamanashi and Holp Shuppan, publishers.

The portrait of Torii Mototada on page 123 originally appeared in *Buke no Kamon to Hatajirushi* (by Kenichi Takahashi, 1972); courtesy of Akita Shoten, publishers.

Our thanks also to the staff and management of Japan's National Diet Library, Division for Interlibrary Services, in Tokyo, for their help in locating and reproducing these portraits.

W.S.W. & G.N.L.

A NOTE ON THE TRANSLATIONS

To preserve the historical character of these translations, all proper names have been written in the traditional Japanese manner, with the family name first.

Dedication

To my children,
Matthew and Michelle,
for their patience

Translation and Introduction by
William Scott Wilson

William Scott Wilson was born in Nashville, Tennessee, in 1944, and grew up in Florida. He is fluent in modern Japanese and has reading knowledge of both classical Japanese and Chinese. He currently holds a master's degree in Japanese language and literature from the University of Washington in Seattle.

Wilson's interest in Japanese culture was sparked on a kayaking expedition along the Japanese coast during 1966 as part of an assignment for *National Geographic*. He returned a year later to live briefly in Japan, but became convinced that a thorough understanding of its people and culture could only be realized by mastering the language. He went to the Monterey Institute of Foreign Studies in California, discovering the inseparable aspect of Japan's warrior tradition within its cultural personality. Wilson also studied a Chinese style of kung fu.

Wilson returned to Japan for some intensive research at Aichi Prefectural University in Nagoya from 1975-77, translating the works of Yamamoto Tsunetomo, which he eventually published as *Hagakure: The Book of the Samurai* (Kodansha International Ltd., 1979). The work is a revealing discussion of the samurai way of life and represents one of the most radical aspects of Japanese thought.

Since August, 1980, Wilson has served as a consular specialist for the Consulate General of Japan in Seattle, heading the Trade Section and advising the Consul on political and economic matters between the U.S. and Japan. Wilson is also at work on a translation of *The Budoshoshinshu*, a classic work on Japanese warrior philosophy by Daidoji Yuzan, written in the early 18th century.

Wilson currently lives in Florida with his wife and two children.

PREFACE

In the spring of 1592, the forces of the once-powerful Takeda clan had been nearly destroyed. Outnumbered by the enemy nearly ten to one, the last feudal lord of the clan fled the provincial capital to Mt. Tenmoku, where he was captured and killed, his once matchless troops in full retreat. Tsuchiya Sozo, a warrior who had been in disfavor for a number of years, came out alone, however, resolved to show his sincerity. With the remark, "I wonder where all the men are who spoke so bravely every day?" he walked out onto the battlefield to die alone in combat.

In the late fall of 1944, a young lieutenant in the Japanese navy named Teshi Haruo was stationed on a small island in the Pacific. One morning in the early hours his post received word by radio that a huge American naval force was on its way through to the Philippines, destroying all Japanese outposts en route. Escape for the lieutenant and his men was not expressed as a possibility. As Lt. Teshi sat listening to the early morning rain, his first thoughts were about his uniform: Was it clean? Had he sincerely shown himself ready to die?

The thread of thought that links men like Tsuchiya Sozo and Lt. Teshi Haruo is a long one, extending to well before the 16th century, and forward today as one of the spiritual foundations of the Japanese people, and consequently of the modern martial arts. It is important to us, not only for understanding one aspect of Japanese history and culture, but also for providing a more solid basis for our own activity—or inactivity—with those around us. Developed by a class that was to rule Japan for nearly 800 years, and interpenetrating Japanese life in so many ways, the samurai spirit is an approach to being in the world that deserves our attention, regardless of what our own particular focus of interest may be.

Who was the warrior and what were his values? There are many sources to which one may turn: histories, novels, or even plays and movies. But these are, essentially, the views of outsiders and, although valid in their own right, do not come from the source itself. In the ninth book of the *Hagakure*, an early 18th-century treatise on the warrior spirit, this story is given:

> The Buddhist priest, Ryozan, wrote down some generalities concerning Lord Takanobu's battles. A certain priest saw this and criticized him saying, "It is inappropriate for a priest to write about a military commander. No matter how successful his writing style may be, since he is not acquainted with military affairs, he is liable to be mistaken in understanding a great general's mind. It is irreverent to pass on misconceptions concerning a famous general to latter generations." (Yamamoto, 1979)

This is the assumption of this book as well, and the guiding principle behind the present translations. To get a complete picture of the Japanese warrior, we must understand how the warrior saw himself.

The materials translated in this book were taken from many textual sources, listed in the bibliography. All of them, however, can be found, with some difference in manuscript forms, in the collection of *Buke no Kakun*, edited by Yoshida Yutaka, and published by the Tokuma Shoten. I am greatly indebted to Mr. Yoshida's notes on the texts and to his clear translations into modern Japanese. I would also like to express my appreciation to Professors Noboru Hiraga and Richard McKinnon who instructed me, against all odds, in the various forms of classical Chinese and Japanese in which the original texts were written, and who assisted me by asking questions concerning the texts for which I rarely seemed to have the proper answers. I am grateful to Akira Takeda, Sally Rutledge and Colleen O'Zora who also gave freely of their time and effort in the progress of the manuscript. Finally, a very special thanks to Marilyn Priestley, who patiently read and re-read parts of my own manuscript, and whose valuable suggestions aided greatly in this production. Any and all mistakes are my own.

—William Scott Wilson
1982

CONTENTS

INTRODUCTION   13

THE MESSAGE OF MASTER GOKURAKUJI   35
  Hojo Shigetoki (1198-1261 A.D.)

THE CHIKUBASHO   45
  Shiba Yoshimasa (1350-1410 A.D.)

THE REGULATIONS OF IMAGAWA RYOSHUN   57
  Imagawa Sadayo (1325-1420 A.D.)

THE SEVENTEEN ARTICLES OF ASAKURA TOSHIKAGE   65
  Asakura Toshikage (1428-1481 A.D.)

THE TWENTY-ONE PRECEPTS OF HOJO SOUN   73
  Hojo Nagauji (1432-1519 A.D.)

THE RECORDED WORDS OF ASAKURA SOTEKI   81
  Asakura Norikage (1474-1555 A.D.)

THE IWAMIZUDERA MONOGATARI   89
  Takeda Shingen (1521-1573 A.D.)

OPINIONS IN NINETY-NINE ARTICLES   99
  Takeda Nobushige (1525-1561 A.D.)

LORD NABESHIMA'S WALL INSCRIPTIONS   113
  Nabeshima Naoshige (1538-1618 A.D.)

THE LAST STATEMENT OF TORII MOTOTADA   119
  Torii Mototada (1539-1600 A.D.)

THE PRECEPTS OF KATO KIYOMASA   127
  Kato Kiyomasa (1562-1611 A.D.)

NOTES ON REGULATIONS   133
  Kuroda Nagamasa (1568-1623 A.D.)

BIBLIOGRAPHY   142

Once I was a gallant with books and a sword . . .
I studied the arts of peace and studied
          the arts of war.
I studied the arts of war and studied the
     arts of peace.

                                        Han-Shan

Learning is something that should be studied
broadly. It is, for example, like the beggar's
bag in which everything from leftover meat to
cold soup is stored.

                              Hosokawa Yusai

INTRODUCTION

"When the world is at peace, a gentleman keeps his sword by his side." —Wu Tsu

literate = Cultured

INTRODUCTION
Description of the Translated Texts

According to Japanese mythology, some thousands of years ago the gods Izanagi and Izanami created the first island of the Japanese archipelago from a "heavenly floating bridge." This they did with a spear. From that time there developed a martial tradition that has been intimately bound up, in one degree or another, with the country's culture in terms of literature, art and ethics, and is a living heritage even today.

The way of life and world-outlook of the Japanese warrior is remarkable, both in the vigor that has sustained him over the centuries, and his balanced view of the complete man as being both martial and literate. Understanding what the warrior meant by these two concepts is important to us in approaching Japanese culture as a whole, and because that understanding may give us a new position to judge our own values as well.

Presented in this book are 12 selections of what might broadly be called *kakun* and *yuikai*, clan precepts and "last statements," from the heads of the Japanese warrior houses to their descendants and clan elders. They range from literal "last statements," such as the letter sent from Torii Mototada to his son on the eve of the destruction of his castle, to precepts meditated upon in the quiet of Buddhist temples by Hojo Shigetoki, or the dictums of Takeda Shingen put into writing years after his death. They are all alike in that they represent the ideals of the warrior class and were written down to help guarantee the perpetuation of the clan; they are statements *from* warriors *to* warriors, without the approval of other classes in mind. They are, therefore, vital and sincere.

The purpose of this introductory essay is to take a broad look at the warriors who wrote and were affected by these precepts in terms of their origin, their society's perception of them, and the systems of thought that were their daily intellectual and emotional bread.

This volume covers a period that could be called the "classical period" of the Japanese warrior; that is, from immediately after the time of Taira no Kiyomori's influence at court in the late 12th century, through the Period of the Warring States, to the beginning of the Tokugawa peace, during which the role of the warrior lost much of its immediacy. It is during this classical period that the warrior's activities in national affairs were greatest in scope, and it is mostly during this time that the genre considered here flourished. Before the 12th century fewer examples of warrior writings seem to exist and, with the Tokugawa peace, the problems of the warrior class changed and were subject more to philosophizing and idealization. Throughout the 600 years in question, the formulation of martial precepts was based directly on experience and was vital to the problem of the continuance of the clan. During the Tokugawa period, however, military affairs ceased to dominate the samurai's life, the great warrior houses were for the most part well established, and the warrior class had to re-examine its values.

The writers presented here represent a broad spectrum of personalities and social standing: from the upper-class members of the *bakufu* (tent government) and hereditary lords (such as Hojo Shigetoki and Shiba Yoshimasa), to the "sudden daimyos" and vassal-generals (like Asakura Toshikage and Torii Mototada), from men who were energetically involved in the world of letters (exemplified by Imagawa Ryoshun), to those who forbade the study of poetry and Noh altogether (like Kato Kiyomasa). In this way, the reader may see the values that remained consistent through many generations and personalities as well as those that changed or were interpreted from a different point of view.

Finally, it should be mentioned that the texts themselves vary substantially in style. The *Regulations of Imagawa Ryoshun* and the *Opinions in Ninety-Nine Articles* were, for example, written in a terse classical Chinese, the latter selection consisting primarily of quotations of older Chinese sources. The *Chikubasho*, on the other hand, was written in a very fluid form of Japanese that reflects the author's high regard for Japanese court life in both style and content. The other selections range in language between these extremes, from the wordiness of Kuroda Nagamasa to the laconic style of Nabeshima Naoshige. Generally, however, these works were written by men who were neither uneducated nor unsophisticated, and follow a grammar that is both readable and remarkably consistent when we consider the dramatic changes in English over the same period of time. Again, they were written less to be enjoyed than to be understood and given heed.

Origin of the Warrior

In Japanese there are several terms that approach the meaning of "warrior," but the closest in usage and feeling is probably the term *bushi* (武士). Breaking down the character *bu* (武) reveals the radical 止, meaning "to stop," and an abbreviation of the radical 戈, "spear." The *Shuo Wen*, an early Chinese dictionary, gives this definition: "*Bu* consists of subduing the weapon and therefore stopping the spear." The *Tso Chuan*, another early Chinese source, goes further:

> *Bu* consists of *bun* (文: literature or letters, and generally the arts of peace) stopping the spear. Bu prohibits violence and subdues weapons . . . it puts the people at peace, and harmonizes the masses.

The radical *shi* (士) on the other hand seems to have originally meant a person who performs some function or who has the ability in some field. Early in Chinese history it came to define the upper class of society, and in the *Book of Han* this definition is given:

> The *shi*, the farmer, the craftsman, and the tradesman are the four professions of the people. He who occupies his rank by means of learning is called a shi.

This should not be misleading, however, because the shi, as the highest of the four classes, brandished the weapons as well as the books. Historically, these shi originated in the late Chou and Warring States Period as the superfluous landed descendants of nobility—well-educated and armed, owing allegiance to no one in particular—farmed out to the provinces because their number overburdened (or worried) the court.

Bushi therefore seems to have meant a man who has the ability to keep the peace, either by literary or military means, but predominantly by the latter. In a book from the Han Period, for example, we find this entry:

> Therefore, the gentleman avoids the three extremities. He avoids the extremity of the pen of the literary man; he avoids the

> extremity of the halberd of the military man; and he avoids the
> extremity of the tongue of the advocate.

The word bushi likely entered the Japanese vocabulary with the general introduction of Chinese learning and was added to the indigenous words, *tsuwamono* and *mononofu*. Its earliest appearance in writing was in the *Shoku Nihongi*, an early history of Japan completed in 797 A.D. In a section of that book covering the year 723, we read:

> Again, the August Personage said, "Literary men and warriors are they whom the nation values."

It is important to keep in mind the connotation of the peaceful arts with this term, for although the bun and the bu were very clearly contrasted, they were at the same time considered essential qualities of the superior man by both the Chinese and Japanese. We will see this distinctly from the Japanese warrior's point of view in these translations.

The other term used for the Japanese military man was *samurai*, written either 士 or 侍. In Chinese, the character 侍 was originally a verb meaning to wait upon or accompany a person in the upper ranks of society, and this is also true of the original term in Japanese, *saburau*. In both countries the terms were nominalized to mean "those who serve in close attendance to the nobility," the pronunciation in Japanese changing to *saburai*. An early reference to this word is found in the *Kokinshu*, the first imperial anthology of poems, completed in the first part of the tenth century.

> *Attendant to nobility*
> *Ask for your master's umbrella.*
> *The dews neath the trees of Miyagino*
> *Are thicker than rain.*
>
> *(Poem 1091)*

From the middle of the Heian Period these attendants served as guardians to the higher nobility and thus carried weapons. As they were taken more and more from the warrior class, saburai became synonymous with bushi almost entirely by the end of the 12th century. As time went on, the word was closely associated with the middle and upper echelons of the warrior class, and especially those who were involved in government or clan administration, or those who were direct vassals.

The origin of the men who carried these names coincided with the development of the *shoen* (estate) system. This system evolved in the late centuries of the first millenium as large rice producing estates were claimed as hereditary possessions of great aristocratic families and thus became exempt from taxation and other inter- ference from the central government. At the same time, the ad- ministration of the public tax-paying domains—still one-half of the tilled land in the late 12th century—gradually fell into the hands of deputies appointed by provincial governors. These lower- ranking deputy positions also tended to become hereditary, and the families who received them often remained in the provinces, extending their households and private lands. As a result of these policies, both the shoen and the public provinces became virtually independent of the central government authorities.

The history of the bushi as a class begins at this point. With the progressive inability of the central government to maintain order in the provinces, both the administrators of public domains and the proprietors of private estates began to develop their own armies to protect their interests in the ensuing struggles over land and title. This movement was actually initiated by the court itself as early as 792 with the introduction of the *kondei* system, a sys- tem that recruited local "physically able" young men, the sons of district chiefs, to keep order in the provinces, and essentially has- tened the abandonment of the concept of a government militia (Lu, 1974). These defense groups, which grew gradually between the ninth and 12th centuries, tended to be organized along family lines, taking in non-related members of the agricultural commun- ity as *ke'nin* (house men) as time went on. As they grew in strength they were often able to discard the aristocratic absentee landlords of the manors they "protected." The need for legiti- macy was fulfilled in the lineage of their leaders who were, if not the descendants of the ancient aristocratic *uji* (clans predating the origin of the warrior class), were descendants of the imperial line itself.

Thus, the Japanese bushi were reminiscent of the Chinese shi who had flourished centuries before. Aristocratic by birth, they were not uneducated; being landholders or administrators of es- tates and often whole provinces, they had income to support the armory and horses necessary to the warrior class.

Eventually, the civil government lost control not only of the provinces, but of the capital itself. In 1156, a succession dispute called the Hogen Disturbance broke out between imperial princes, and leaders of the two major bushi clans, the Taira and Minamoto, were called upon to back one pretender or another. The result of the clash was the temporary emergence of the Taira and eclipse of the Minamoto, but more importantly, the beginning of warrior rule: Taira Kiyomori, the head of his clan, not only took military control of Kyoto, but also began to dominate the court as well. The Taira in turn were crushed in 1185 by a re-emergence of the Minamoto, and with this event bushi rule became complete. The leader of the Minamoto forces, Yoritomo, established the bakufu. This organization in one form or another would be the basic government apparatus in Japan for the next 700 years.

The new warrior government strengthened its already powerful position through economic means. With the defeat of Taira, Yoritomo was able to claim extensive holdings expropriated from the defeated enemy, many of which he used as rewards, either as private estates or administrative appointments, for those who had supported him. This action broadened the warriors' economic base considerably, and created a vassalage for Yoritomo and later the bakufu in general. The warrior was now entirely in control.

The image of the aristocratic warrior described in the early chronicles tells only part of the story. Although many of its leaders came from aristocratic or even imperial lineage, the ranks of the samurai class were bolstered by the low class *ashigaru* (foot soldier), who did not share the cultural background or economic means of his betters. Still, some of these men and their families came up through the ranks rewarded for ability or feats of courage. They became, if not aristocrats, upper-class warriors and generals. This phenomenon was most pronounced during the Warring States Period, and the extreme example would be that of Toyotomi Hideyoshi, who rose from a very low estate to be the most powerful ruler in the country. Ironically, this was the same man who, beginning with the famous "sword hunt" of 1588 and through an edict in 1591, closed the social mobility by which he and others had risen, enclosing Japanese society within the four classes of warriors, farmers, artisans and merchants.

Finally, it was the warrior class that in large part carried on the cultural heritage received from the fading court aristocracy. From the time of Taira, the temptation to stay in the capital and dally in literary or other cultural affairs had been detrimental to the clan's survival and even to the warrior class' ruling position, and the various leaders were able to deal with this problem with varying degrees of success. At least some cultural attainment was considered important by almost all of the great warrior leaders, and a rise in the power or social status of a warrior or clan was usually accompanied by a corresponding effort to attain similar heights in the world of culture. The examples of the castle towns at Ichijo-gatani and Odawara built by the Asakura and the later Hojo demonstrate this tendency to a remarkable degree. Under this impetus and the image of the correct balance of bun and bu, the ideal of the scholar-warrior would survive even after the battles were long over. It would be a mistake, however, to think that all samurai were lettered. For although a more democratic education among the warriors gained momentum as time went on, it had certainly not been fully realized—despite the social position of the class as a whole—even by the late 17th century.

The View of the Warrior in Literature

The character of the warrior appears throughout the literature of Japan and studying this literature makes it possible to examine the warrior as he was seen through the eyes of his contemporary observers.

The warrior first appears in the *Kojiki*, Japan's oldest extant book, compiled in 712 by a learned aristocrat as a sort of national history of the Yamato Court, and reaches back to the earliest memories of the Japanese people. It may be mentioned in passing that the first emperor recorded by the *Kojiki* was named Jimmu (神武), or Divine Warrior, supposed to have flourished around the seventh century, B.C. Although the chapters concerned with Emperor Jimmu deal in part with his military conquests, it is the accounts of his descendant, Yamato Takeru, or the Brave of Yamato, that we are given the picture of the individual warrior and his character.

Diction in the *Kojiki* and elsewhere indicates that Yamato Takeru may have been considered as an emperor himself, but he is usually regarded as the brave and somewhat wild son of the Emperor Keiko, and the pacifier of "the unruly dieties and unsubmissive people" of the East and West (Philippi, 1968). Although he began his career in the signal manner of slaughtering his elder brother as he went to the privy, Yamato Takeru spent his life traveling the length and breadth of the country in military conquests at his father's command. Though rough and cunning in his dealings with the enemy, he is given sympathetic treatment in the *Kojiki*, portrayed as a filial son lamenting his own father's distance and, perhaps, fear of him. On his way to conquering the tribes of the East, he says to his aunt:

> "Is it because the emperor wishes me to die soon? Why did he dispatch me to attack the evil people of the West? Then when I came back, why did he dispatch me once more after only a short while, without giving me troops, to subdue the evil people of . . . the East? In view of all of this, he must wish me to die soon."
> Thus saying, he lamented and cried. (Philippi, 1968)

The *Kojiki*, moreover, assigns to him the composition of several poems. Upon the slaying of Izumo Takeru (after tricking him into wearing a bladeless sword) he recites:

> *The many-clouds-rising*
> *Izumo Takeru*
> *Wears a Sword*
> *With many vines wrapped around it,*
> *But no blade inside, alas.*

Other poems are addressed to loved ones, his homeland, and even a pine tree, but his last poem, composed as he lay dying, attests to his martial calling:

> *Next to the maiden's*
> *Sleeping place*
> *I left*
> *The sabre, the sword—*
> *Alas, that sword.*

a poem prophetic of the high regard to be given the Japanese sword in a much later age.

Yamato Takeru may be considered the rough ideal of the Japanese warrior to come. He is sincere and loyal, slicing up his father's enemies "like melons," unbending and yet not unfeeling, as can be seen in his laments for lost wives and homeland, and in his willingness to combat the enemy alone. Most important, his portrayal in the *Kojiki* indicates that the ideal of harmonizing the literary with the martial may have been an early trait of Japanese civilization, appealing to the Japanese long before its introduction from Confucian China.

Whether the depiction of Yamato Takeru is a close replica of the warrior in first-century Japan, a creation of eighth-century aristocrats, or some combination of the two, is a matter of conjecture. What is certain is that by the end of the tenth century, military personnel were no longer considered fit subjects for literature by the court, at least at any length. While officers of the palace guard and capital police were elected from the aristocratic circles, these posts were no more than formalities and those who filled them "would have been incredulous and horrified if the Ministry (of War) had asked them to perform any military duties" (Morris, 1969). The real warrior was indelibly connected with the provinces, and those who lived in the provinces were considered barbarians. The city of Heian-kyo was the center of all things that mattered, and for most of the people who lived there the appointment of a post at any distance from the capital was considered a misfortune.

This was certainly the prevailing attitude at the time of Lady Murasaki, the author of the *Tale of Genji*, Japan's oldest novel. Her unflattering description of Tayu no Gen, the Lord-Lieutenant of Tsukushi, was apparently typical of the regard in which even the highest-ranking military men were held. Beyond having "the power (which he frequently exercised) of assuming the most repulsively ferocious expression," his style of calligraphy—the art that was considered above all others to manifest breeding in Heian times—"was not an agreeable one, being very tortuous and affected" (Waley, 1935). He is generally dismissed as a "coarse and unscrupulous barbarian," and Tamarazura, the sad object of his affections, is lamented as "being wasted in this barbarous and sequestered land," which in this case happened to be Kyushu but could just as easily have been a short distance outside the Heian-kyo city limits.

At any rate, the contempt of the courtiers for the warrior is rendered conspicuous in the *Tale of Genji* by the absence of nearly any mention of him at all. The courtiers' feelings are ironically put into the very mouth of Tayu no Gen, and his own words perhaps summarize their prejudices most clearly. After "a long period of meditation" he has produced a poem judged favorable only by himself, and goes on to say:

> "I expect you look upon me as a very uncultivated, provincial person. And so I should be if I were at all like the other people around here. But I've been very fortunate; you would not find many men even at the City who have had a better education than I. You'd be making a great mistake if you set me down as a plain, countrified sort of man. As a matter of fact there's nothing I have not studied." He would very much have liked to try his hand at a second poem; but his stock of ideas was exhausted and he was obliged to take leave. (Waley, 1935)

The judgment passed on warriors like Tayu no Gen would not always remain so harsh and ironic. Centuries of stale court life gradually introduced a transition period in which the warrior, if not admired outright, was looked upon with wonder and fascination for his abilities and way of life.

We can find a hint of this new outlook in the *Konjaku Monogatari*, a collection of tales on varying subjects compiled, shaky tradition has it, sometime after 1106 from the collected stories of one Minamoto Takakuni, a member of the court. In the 25th chapter of this collection are stories relating the character and deeds of the rising bushi class, and one of them, though rather long, is worth relating here in full:

> A long time ago there was a warrior named Minamoto no Yorinobu Asson, who was the former governor of Kawachi. Hearing that there was a man in Azuma who had an excellent horse, he dispatched a servant there to ask for it. The owner found it difficult to refuse this request, and commended the horse to Yorinobu's care. On the way back to the capital there was a horse thief who saw this animal and, being struck with avarice, made up his mind to steal it. Although he followed the party secretly during their progress up to the capital, the warriors who accompanied the horse were not negligent at all; and the thief, unable to obtain it on the way, approached the city, too. The horse, on its arrival, was put into Yorinobu's stables.
>
> About this time, Yorinobu's son Yoriyoshi, was informed that they had just brought up a good horse from Azuma to his father's place. Yoriyoshi thought, "That horse will probably be handed over to somebody of no account. Before that happens, I'll go over and look at it, and, if it really is a good one, ask for it myself." And he went to his father's house.
>
> Though there was heavy rainfall, Yoriyoshi was unhampered by it in his desire for the horse and went on through the night. ... His father thought that he had heard about the arrival of the horse and had come to ask for it, but before Yoriyoshi said any-

thing, Yorinobu said, "I have heard that a horse arrived today from Azuma, but have not yet seen it. Its former owner has said that it is a good one. As tonight is dark, we won't be able to see a thing; so tomorrow morning take a look, and if it strikes your fancy, take it right away." Yoriyoshi was glad that this was said before he made his request, and replied, "Well, then tonight I'll stay here, and tomorrow take a look," and stayed over. During the evening they talked and, as the night grew late, the father went to sleep and Yoriyoshi also laid down beside him.

During this time, the sound of rain falling continued incessantly. In the middle of the night, taking advantage of the gloom of the rain, the horse thief made his entrance, pulled the horse outside, and made off. Just at that time, someone yelled from the direction of the stables, "A thief has taken the horse that was brought in last evening!" Yorinobu heard this voice faintly, and without asking the sleeping Yoriyoshi if he had heard it, got up just as he was, tucked in his clothing, shouldered a quiver of arrows, ran to the stables and himself led out a horse, put a plain saddle on it, mounted, and set out alone in chase in the direction of Mt. Ausaka. . . .

Yoriyoshi, too, had heard that voice, and, thinking in the same manner as his father, had made no explanations to him. He had slept fully dressed without loosening his sash, and now he got up just as he was. Like his father, he shouldered a quiver of arrows and went off in chase alone toward Mt. Ausaka.

The thief, mounted on the stolen horse, thought that he had now managed his escape, and, in a watery place at the foot of Mt. Ausaka, let the horse splash slowly through the water. Yorinobu heard this, and, though it was dark and he had no knowledge of Yoriyoshi's whereabouts, yelled out, "Shoot! There he is!" just as though he had made detailed arrangements beforehand. Before the words finished leaving his mouth, a bow twanged and, along with the sound of the arrow hitting something, the sound of empty stirrups could be heard as the horse ran. Again, Yorinobu said, "The thief has been shot down. Bring the horse back home quickly." Saying only this, he returned without waiting for the horse to be brought in. Yoriyoshi then went out to find the horse, and returned. . . . Returning to his home, Yorinobu made nothing of the preceding events, and in fact informed no one, but as it was still night, went back to bed just like before. Yoriyoshi put the returned horse in the care of the servants, and he, too, went back to bed.

Later, at daybreak, Yorinobu came out and, without commending his son on the exceptional way in which the horse had been saved or on the way he had shot so well, simply said, "Take out the horse," and the horse was taken out. Yoriyoshi saw that it was truly a fine horse and said, "Well then, I'll take it, please," and took the horse away. . . .

This is clearly a way of thinking of extraordinary people, and this story has been told to show that the warrior's mind is like this. . . .

The story fairly well speaks for itself. In it is revealed the narrator's admiration and wonder at the warriors' character, their silent communication and self-reliance, and the way their courage and bowmanship seemed as normal to them as waking and sleeping. And though this story was told only 100 years after the time of Lady Murasaki, it represents a great change in attitude from centuries of courtly disdain, and prefigures the epic that was to represent the ideals of the warrior for ages to come.

The *Heike Monogatari* is one of the longest and most beautifully composed of the genre called *gunki monogatari*, or war chronicles. Although written in prose, it has much in common stylistically with poetry as it was originally chanted aloud, and at times breaks into the familiar 7-5, 7-5 pattern of Japanese lyrics. It is epic both in that it is a poetic narrative recounting the lives of heroic personages, and that it embodies a nation's conception of its own history and character. Clearly depicted throughout the *Heike Monogatari* is the ideal of the cultivated warrior. This ideal is symbolized in the character 武 or *uruwashii*, meaning a situation of balance and harmony between the exterior pattern or beauty 文, and the interior essence or substance 武. Men who possess this quality will be as accomplished in the world of the arts as in the world of martial skill and courage.

Atsumori, for example, is a young Taira chieftain who is captured while returning to his abandoned camp for his prized flute, for which he was said to have great talent. Though only a youth, Atsumori is a perfect example of the aristocratic warrior, and the narrative describes at length his elegant appearance:

The warrior wore armour laced with light green silk cords over a twilled silk battle robe decorated with an embroidered design of cranes. On his head was a gold-horned helmet. He carried a sword in a gold-studded sheath and a bow bound with red-lacquered rattan. His quiver held a set of black and white feathered arrows, the center of each feather bearing a black mark. He rode a dappled gray outfitted with a gold-studded saddle. (Kitagawa and Tsuchida, 1975)

When challenged, Atsumori quickly accepts and is just as quickly overpowered by his stronger adversary. He refuses to identify himself to the lower-ranking man, however, and tells his captor:

"I cannot declare myself to such as you. So take my head and show it to the others. They will identify me." (Kitagawa and Tsuchida, 1975)

Elegant, and yet unwincing at the prospect of death, he has lived and died as both courtier and manly warrior.

Taira no Tadanori, "a man of great strength and quick reflexes," is another warrior described in the *Heike Monogatari* who returns to face danger, in this case for literary considerations. He returns to the capital abandoned by his clan to visit his old poetry teacher, Shunzei, and leave a final poem. Later, at the battle of Ichi-no-tani, he is left by his retainers to meet his end, which he does bravely in battle. After he is killed, a poem is found attached to his quiver:

> *When the day is done*
> *I take a tree for my lodge.*
> *On my weary way,*
> *Lying under its broad boughs,*
> *A flower is my sole host.*

And, at the declaration of his death,

Friends and foes alike wet their sleeves with tears and said, "What a pity! Tadanori was a great general, pre-eminent in the arts of both sword and poetry." (Kitagawa and Tsuchida, 1975)

The warriors in the *Heike Monogatari* served as models for the educated warriors of later generations, and the ideals depicted by them were not assumed to be beyond reach. Rather, these ideals were vigorously pursued in the upper echelons of warrior society and recommended as the proper form of the Japanese man of arms. With the *Heike Monogatari*, the image of the Japanese warrior in literature came to its full maturity.

The Warrior's View of Literature

Prior to the 12th century, there is little evidence for the historical accuracy of the idealized warriors portrayed in the *Heike Monogatari* and other literary works. With the organization of the military bakufu however, the warrior took a more active—and documented—role in society. It is from about this time that the kakun and yuikai begin to appear—statements from the warriors themselves such as those represented in this book. Many of the selections in this volume deal with the question of the value of literature to the warrior.

Perhaps the most outspoken of the writers translated here on the value of cultural attainment is Shiba Yoshimasa (1350-1410). Shiba was involved in political and military struggles throughout his life, but still found time for the study of poetry, calligraphy and court football (*kemari*). His best-known work, the *Chikubasho*, was composed in an elegant classical Japanese style when he was 33, and assures the reader that the ideal of the cultured warrior did not die with the *Heike Monogatari:*

> When a man has ability in the arts, the depth of his heart can be conjectured and the mind of his clan surmised. No matter how noble a family one may be born into or how good-looking he may be, when people are picking up the manuscripts for recitation of chants, thinking over the rhymes for making poetry or tuning up their instruments, how deplorable it must be to be among people reciting linked verse and to have to make some excuse for one's inability, or to sit chin in hands while others are playing music together.

Or this:

> The man whose profession is arms should calm his mind and look into the depths of others. Doing so is likely the best of the martial arts.
>
> It is fairly certain that most ordinary people have picked up the *Genji Monogatari* or Sei Shonagon's *Makura Soshi* and read through them any number of times. There is nothing like these books for the instruction of man's behavior and the bearing of the quality of his heart. Reading them, one will naturally be able to recognize a man with soul.

Here is evidenced an almost direct connection in Shiba's mind between ability in the cultural arts, the depth of one's heart, the martial arts, and the study of the classical literature of the Heian Period. Shiba has remarkably little else to say about military matters in the *Chikubasho*, but rather enjoins the young men of his clan to live ethical lives and to develop their sensitivities and abilities in cultural refinements.

Another general who stressed cultural attainment in the life of the warrior was Imagawa Ryoshun (1325-1420). He is well-known for having studied poetry under the great master of the Nijo school, the courtier Yoshimoto, and for composing it happily on his way to the military pacification of Kyushu. After years of campaigning and subsequent administration of that island, he returned to Suruga, turning his energies primarily to literary affairs. The following selections from his *Regulations* clearly manifest Imagawa's feelings concerning these matters:

> It is natural that training in the martial arts is the Way of the Warrior, but it is most important to put them into actual practice. First, it is written in the Confucian classics as well as in the military writings that in protecting the country, if one is ignorant of the study of literature he will be unable to govern.
>
> Just as the Buddha preached the various laws in order to save all living beings, one must rack one's brains and never depart from the Ways of both Warrior and Literary Man.

Although it is not written in the fluid language of Shiba Yoshimasa, the message here is almost the same: a complete man will be a master of both the arts of peace and the arts of war; when lacking the literary, the military cannot be sustained.

Not all warriors advocated the study of literature as wholeheartedly as did Shiba Yoshimasa and Imagawa Ryoshun. However, the ideal of harmonizing the roles of the martial and literary man remained present throughout the medieval period of Japanese history. Kato Kiyomasa (1562-1611), in the following order to all of his samurai "regardless of rank," endorsed learning but placed strict limits on what was to be studied:

> One should put forth effort in matters of Learning. One should read books concerning military matters, and direct his attention exclusively to the virtues of loyalty and filial piety. Reading Chinese poetry, linked verse, and *waka* is forbidden. One will surely become womanized if he gives his heart knowledge of such elegant and delicate refinements. Having been born into the house of a warrior, one's intentions should be to grasp the long and short swords and to die.

Concerning other refinements, Kato had this to say:

> The practice of Noh dancing is absolutely forbidden. . . . A samurai who practices dancing—which is outside of the martial arts—should be ordered to commit *seppuku*.

Kato was a soldier's soldier and a blacksmith's son, probably receiving little courtly education, thus representing the opposite end of the spectrum from Shiba and Imagawa in both upbringing and outlook. Though their interpretations of the concept of learning may differ, it was never doubted by any one of these men that this ideal was an integral part of the warrior's life.

Beginning in 1600, and lasting for the next 250 years, Japan was at peace under the administration of a bakufu government. The economy expanded, and it was perhaps indicative of the times that the shogun surrounded himself with not only military men and scholars but even merchants. Under these circumstances many members of the warrior class found themselves in an environment for which their training as warriors had left them unprepared, and from the amount of attention devoted in writings of the times to the question of what is a samurai, it is evident that it was a period during which the man of arms had to reassess himself. The bakufu itself was not ignorant of this problem, and as early as 1615 issued the *Buke Sho-Hatto*, or Rule for the Military Houses, which as its first item, stated:

> The study of literature and the practice of the military arts, including archery and horsemanship, must be cultivated diligently.
>
> "On the left hand literature, on the right hand use of arms" was the rule of the ancients. Both must be pursued concurrently.
> (Lu, 1974)

Among those who worried about the problems of the samurai was Yamaga Soko (1622-1685), a member of the warrior class and a student of Neo-Confucianism. Yamaga was deeply concerned with the warrior's continued inactivity in peaceful times, and attempted to find an ethical definition of the warrior. In his theory of *Shido* (a less radical theory than bushido), he defined the warrior as an example of Confucian purity to the other classes of society, and as punisher of those who would stray from its path. To Yamaga, the samurai must become a sort of Warrior-Sage, and it was toward the perfection of this transcendent ideal that he directed much of his writings.

This direction of thinking, however, which was typical of the scholars of the Edo Period in its tendency toward speculation, goes beyond the precepts considered here. The kakun and yuikai, written largely during or immediately after times of military unrest, were more homilies than philosophical statements, aimed not toward the sagehood of the individual samurai but toward the perpetuation of the clan. Although the Edo Period lasted 250 years and was a period of warrior rule, it was a time when the warrior's role was more idealized than realized. As an era of peace, it perhaps encouraged philosophical speculation; as an era of doubt, it is little wonder that the study of *jitsugaku* (practical studies)—a study of his true function—was a major concern of that speculation.

Basic Reading and Religious Background

Most often mentioned as suggested reading material in the warrior's own precepts are the Confucian classics, and more specifically the Four Books: the *Analects*, the *Great Learning*, the *Doctrine of the Mean*, and the *Mencius*. Takeda Nobushige's *Ninety-Nine Articles*, which includes examples of what was considered proper reading for the educated warrior, lists the *Analects of Confucius* as one of the principle texts of study.

Basically a philosophy of humanism, Confucianism places much emphasis on education, rationalism, sincerity of action, and the relationships of people involved in society, rather than spiritual affairs or speculation on life after death. In Confucianism, it is man "that can make the Way great," rather than "the Way that can make man great" (*Analects*, 15:28). Good government is considered to be founded on virtue and example rather than on military might or force, and the perfect man is considered a man of virtue rather than profit. In terms of human relationships, Confucianism stresses filial piety in the home and fidelity within society at large.

The *Analects* consists of many short aphorisms which afford an approach to the core of Confucianism. No doubt its readers in the warrior class extrapolated their own interpretations of the Confucian doctrine by selected readings. The following are some selections that they may have found most attractive.

> The Ways of the gentleman are three ... in humanity, he has no anxieties; in wisdom, he has no confusion; and in courage, he has no fears. (14:30)

It also teaches contentment with poverty and simplistic living:

> The Master said, "Having plain food to eat, water to drink, and a bent arm as one's pillow ... there is surely also enjoyment in this!" (7:15)

This is certainly consistent with campaign life. Strict adherence to rites and decorum are advocated, and courtesy is so esteemed that in the *Hagakure* we read that the warrior is respected "precisely because he has correct manners."

The *Analects* also teaches respect for poetry:

> If you do not study Poetry, you will not be able to speak. (16: 13)

One can see here a hint of the harmonizing of the bun and the bu. Confucius, it should be remembered, belonged to the class of the knights-errant. Su Ma-ch'ien, in the *Shih Chi*, has Confucius say:

> I have heard that when a man has literary business, he will always take military preparations; and when he has military business, he will always take literary preparations.

The true gentleman should also have a warrior-like self-reliance based on his own perfection:

> The gentleman seeks things in himself; the inferior man seeks things in others. (*Analects* 15:21)

> The gentleman is without anxiety and without fear. . . . When he looks into himself and finds nothing vexatious, how will there be anxiety, how will there be fear? (12:4)

But perfection should be tempered with humility:

> Meng Chih-fan was not boastful. In a retreat, he took up the rear position. As he was about to enter the gate, he whipped his horse and said, "It's not that I dared to be the last, the horse just wouldn't go." (6:15)

The warriors, whose functions extended into broader administrative areas as Court rites and ceremonies became empty formalities, were men who had real problems to solve. As warriors, their calling was one of life and death; after 1221, their governing duties extended throughout most of the country. From the late 12th century and especially through the Warring States Period, men from the bushi class found it necessary to establish in themselves both the arts of war and the arts of peace as necessary conditions for the survival of themselves and their clans. In the *Great Learning* they found a key to this survival in the Confucian ideal of self-cultivation, and the connection between the single-mindedness of the individual and the ruling of the country:

> Only by moving with focus can one have stability. Only by being stable can one have peace. Only by having peace can one be secure. Only in security can one deliberate. And only with deliberation will one be able to obtain.

And before governing others one must learn to govern himself:

> Those who desired to govern their states would first put their

families in order. And those who desired to put their families in
order would first discipline themselves.

Thus, the general measure of the *Great Learning* is that virtue
works on a vertical slide, and for the warrior this meant moving
from the individual leader down through the entire province. This
also applied to the clan as a whole:

If one family has humanity, the entire state will become humane.
If one family has courtesy, the entire state will become courte-
ous. But if one man is grasping and perverse, the entire country
will be brought into rebellion.

Vital to the concept of self-control and achievement is the virtue of sincerity. This sincerity has a sort of transcendent, even
mystical quality, akin to single-mindedness and somehow more
connected with the man whose life is on the line in the battlefield
than with the rank-conscious courtier embroiled in palace in-
trigues. The warrior could afford little equivocating, and the
principle of sincerity offered him the way to break through his
problems. He was taught to be as sincere to himself as to others;
a policy leading to internal as well as external honesty, an honesty
to one's enemies as well as to one's allies. In the *Doctrine of the
Mean* we find:

Sincerity is the Way of Heaven; making oneself sincere is the Way
of man. Sincerity hits what is right without effort, and obtains
(understanding) without thinking.

Confucianism offered a sound and comprehensive system within
which the warrior could go about his temporal affairs. Buddhism,
on the other hand, though introduced to Japan about the same
time as Confucianism (the sixth or seventh centuries), was at first
of interest only to the nobility, some of whom admired it more
for its pageantry than for its philosophy. In the 12th and 13th
centuries, however, the priests Eisai and Dogen brought a kind of
Buddhism called *Zen* to Japan that had been developing in China
since the early T'ang Dynasty (618-906). It required no ceremonies or academic studies, and put extreme reliance on individual
willpower and self-discipline. It was a Buddhism of action and intuition rather than intellectualization, of moving forward rather
than dwelling on the past. This was very attractive to the man on
the battlefield.

Along with the values of self-reliance, asceticism, and single-mindedness (all of which were shared in common with Confucianism), Zen laid great emphasis on self-denial, or transcending life and death as a condition of attaining spiritual salvation. The warrior's duty, of course, was to fight and die, and in this transcendent posture, Zen offered him the spiritual training necessary to carry out his duty unflinchingly.

Zen, however, occupied the paradoxical position of relying on intuition ("not standing on scriptures") and yet teaching a respect for learning and even acting as its vehicle. Here again, the warrior found the principle of rugged and manly discipline harmonized with the literary world.

Not all warriors belonged to the Zen sect of Buddhism, of course, but it was Zen that ultimately had the greatest effect on warrior society.

Finally, the Chinese military classics should be mentioned, due both to their immediacy to the warrior's profession and to the allusion given them in the precepts. Some of these classics may date back as far as the fifth and sixth centuries B.C., and have long held the respect of not only military men but scholars and poets as well. Military strategies for the most part, they were read attentively by the great Japanese campaigners; among the writers here they are mentioned by Imagawa Ryoshun and Kato Kiyomasa, and quoted extensively by Takeda Nobushige. Aside from their purely tactical advice, however, they must have helped in the formation of warrior attitudes with principles such as the following:

> Therefore, it is a functional military law that one does not rely on the enemy not coming, but relies on the fact that he himself is waiting; one does not rely on the enemy not attacking, but relies on the fact that he himself is unassailable. (*Sun Tzu* 9:11)

> When the world is at peace, a gentleman keeps his sword by his side. (*Wu Tzu*—Griffith, 1977)

Conclusion

The Japanese warriors responded differently to these various influences from diverse places in time, circumstance, and personality. Underlying these differences, however, two basic attitudes remain fairly constant throughout: that if the advice given is followed, the individual will gain in character, and the province and the clan will be properly maintained. More often than not, the assumption is that the latter depends absolutely on the former.

Thus, if the warrior was encouraged to study poetry or letters or even religion, it was less from an academic point of view than a pragmatic one; the more well-rounded and total the man is, the better he will be able to cope with his surroundings. "Learning," said Takeda Shingen, "is not only reading books, but rather something we study to integrate with our own way of life."

As we have seen, a balance of literary arts and the martial arts was considered ideal, encouraged by Confucianism and substantiated by the Buddhist scholars. The example of the Court was forever before the warrior, both as an ideal of the glittering world of letters, and as a warning of the impotence incurred when the sword is put down completely in favor of the pen. Concerning this dichotomy, Kuroda Nagamasa wrote:

> The arts of peace and the arts of war are like the two wheels of
> a cart which, lacking one, will have difficulty in standing.

How well the warriors were able to sustain that balance may be judged, in part, by these precepts compared with the lives of their writers.

One may read these precepts, then, from different perspectives. They may be read as documentary evidence of warrior attitudes in certain times and places, or from a strictly literary point of view, or again, as material giving fresh and direct insight into some of the most interesting men in Japanese history. There is a current running throughout these readings, however, that bears directly on ourselves and our own values: the Way of the Warrior is the way to the total man and the journey to a fuller self. In our own specialized culture, the scholar and the poet are too often identified with the dove, while the soldier is depicted as too martial and unfeeling; their camps are mutually exclusive. The leaders of the Japanese warrior class attempted to span that gulf. If they did not attain that ideal, they did maintain and preserve it while living and acting in the world with a broader point of view than that with which we ourselves might claim.

THE MESSAGE OF
MASTER GOKURAKUJI

"If one will fix his heart in such a way and assist the world and its people, he will have the devotion of the men who see and hear of him."

THE MESSAGE OF MASTER GOKURAKUJI

Hojo Shigetoki
(1198-1261 A.D.)

Hojo Shigetoki, the third son of Hojo Yoshitoki, was only five years old when the Hojo clan became shogunal regents under his grandfather, Hojo Tokimasa.

In 1223, he became the Military Governor of the province of Suruga, and in 1230 was appointed the Shogun's Deputy in Kyoto, an office he filled until 1247. With the defeat of the rival Miura clan in that year, Hojo went to Kamakura to assist the Regent, Tokiyori, in the organization of the bakufu. In 1256 he shaved his head and became a monk, retiring to the Ritsu-sect temple that he had established, the Gokurakuji, where he spent his remaining years in seclusion and contemplation. He had lived through a period that saw the consolidation of both political and economic power for the warrior class, a period of relative calm when compared to the Gempei wars that preceded it, and the revolt of the Ashikaga clan that was to follow.

Hojo was known for the selfless help he provided his higher-placed relatives in the administration of the bakufu, and for his deep faith in Buddhism. Of his writings, two are extant: The Precepts of the Lord of Rokuhara, *a set of practical precepts he wrote for his son, Nagatoki, in 1247; and* The Message of Gokurakuji-dono, *from which the present text is taken, written sometime after 1256 for his son and the house elders in general. This latter consists of 100 articles written in the* kanamajiri *style, and is basically concerned with man's moral duties and the ideal behavior for leaders of the warrior class. The predominant tone of the work is a Buddhist sympathy for all living beings and an awareness of the functions of karma. Women, children, and those of lower social standing are to be treated kindly and with regard, and even the concept of loyalty to superiors is dealt with more in a religious sense than a Confucian one.*

The Message of Gokurakuji-dono *reflects the religious feelings that seem to have been common with the Hojo family, and in this respect is probably the least secular of all the precepts presented in this book.*

The Message Of Master Gokurakuji

To begin with, although it is presumptuous of me to say so, the relationship of parent and child exists inasmuch as their bond in a previous existence was no shallow one. Truly, the impermanence of the world is like a dream within a dream. The men we saw yesterday are not here today, and the existence of those today will be in peril tomorrow. Man's fate does not wait his breathing in and breathing out. The sun that rose in the morning sinks behind the mountain ridge in the evening, and the moon of the night before marks the beginning of the day. The blooming flowers only wait for the enticement of the storm. From these it can be seen that transience is not limited to man. And, although it would at least seem determined that old men pass away and young men live on, the fact is that death has no respect for age; and when one truly thinks about it, one cannot rely simply on youth in this uncertain world. This being so, should we not want to be remembered by others and cultivate our minds?

Thinking that there are few opportunities to speak of such things directly, I am writing them down in this manner. One should read this carefully at his leisure as a diversion, and it should not be lent to others. Should I not be able to escape the round of birth and death again this time, even though I am reborn in innumberable successions it will be difficult to meet with you again, and these writings may be considered as reminiscences of the world into which I was fated to be born.

First are the articles one should think over in his heart and put into practice with his body.

One should worship the gods and Buddhas morning and night, and maintain a heart of faith. The gods grant power to a man according to his respect for them, and he maintains his fate according to their blessings. Thus, when coming before the gods and Buddhas, for better ability in this world one should ask to be granted an upright heart. In this way he will be esteemed in this world and born in the Western Paradise in the next, and this is a fine thing. One should understand this principle well.

When one is serving officially or in the master's court, he should not think of a hundred or a thousand people, but should consider only the importance of the master. Nor should he draw the line at his own life or anything else he considers valuable. Even if the master is being phlegmatic and one goes unrecognized, he should know that he will surely have the divine protection of the gods and Buddhas. While in the midst of duties, one should keep this principle in mind concerning service at the master's court, too. To think of receiving the blessings of the master without fulfilling the duties of court service is no different from trying to cross a rough sea without a boat.

One should not disregard, even in jest, the instructions of his parents. Although there should be no one, as a parent, who would instruct his child for the worse, the children who use their parents' instructions are rare.

Turning this over in our minds, with our eyes closed, let us think this over well. How sorrowful must be the heart of the lamenting parent who sees his child turning bad. It could certainly be said that this child is unfilial. And how happy the heart must be of the rejoicing parent who sees his child being good. This can certainly be said to be filial piety.

One should listen with a calm mind to what one's parents say, even if what they say is erroneous.

It is said that when the elderly become enfeebled, they enter their second childhood. Their hair becomes white, their foreheads become wrinkled, and their hips bend like a bow of catalpa wood. When looking in the mirror their image has changed, and one would doubt that they are the same person. The person who comes once in a great while to visit pays his respects and goes home, and there is truly no one who comes to stay awhile. The elderly person's mind has certainly changed from how it was in the past; he cannot remember the things that he has heard, and forgets what he has seen. He feels resentment in the things he should rejoice in, and rejoices in the things he should resent. These things are all in the nature of the elderly.

Understanding this well, one should first have sympathy with what his elderly parents have said, and not turn his back on them. When the way passed by one's parents has been long and their destination at hand, one may wonder how much longer he will listen to such words as theirs. At this time he should follow their dictums by all means. This will surely come to one's own mind after *he* has become old.

If there is some discord between one's parents and another person, if one will placate the other party there is nothing that should go awry. If there is something between one's self and one's parents, he should at any rate follow his parents' instructions. If he does not, he will have nothing but regret after the sad leave-taking, and will wish that he had obeyed them while they were still alive.

When one is in a place where people are gathered together, and fish, fruit, and the like are being served, even if he is partaking of this himself he should do so in a manner that others may have more. Nevertheless, one should not let others be aware of this.

When one is serving food, it will not do to serve one's self more than the guest. Nor should one, with the above in mind, serve small portions. He should serve the proper amount.

When passing by the quarters of women of high rank, one

should pass by without looking around repeatedly. In fact, one should not look at all. And one should make strict instructions to those of lower rank accompanying him that they should not look either.

There is error in the midst of conforming to reason, and reason in the midst of error. One should understand this well.

Error in the midst of reason is when one is so convinced of his own reasonableness that he pushes his opinion forward, not to the extent that it will cause injury to himself, but to the extent that it may cause another man to lose his life. This is error in the midst of reason.

It is truly regrettable that a person will treat a man who is valuable to him well, and a man who is worthless to him poorly.

Reason in the midst of error is when a man is about to lose his life and one comes to his aid without disclosing the thousands of mistakes that may be involved. This is reason in the midst of error. If one will fix his heart in such a way and assist the world and its people, he will have the devotion of the men who see and hear of him. Moreover, how much will the joy be of the man who has been helped? And even if the person helped and the people around him do not rejoice, one will have kindled the devotion of the gods and Buddhas, and will have protection in this life and assistance in the life to come.

Concerning matters of dress, no matter by whom one is being seen he should not appear shabbily, and even if he is mixing with the lower classes he should dress to a moderate extent. When often in the midst of humble people, one should not repeatedly dress splendidly. A person with sensitivity will be prudent in this matter.

When one of one's companions has been rebuked by the master, one should find it more lamentable than if he himself had been rebuked. If the master should tell him about his companion's error, he should mediate well for the man. For even if the master does not agree with him at the time, it will impress him well later on.

At the time of merry-making, one should be very prudent about joining in with a superior who is riding a wave of amusement. This sort of thing is what is called "a crow imitating a cormorant." No matter how much one may be letting loose or how drunk he may be, he should be very careful of his demeanor when he is in the same place as a superior. No matter how raucous one may get, he should be very aware of his surroundings.

It is truly regrettable that a person will treat a man who is valuable to him well, and a man who is worthless to him poorly. Even dogs and beasts will be glad and wag their tails when someone treats them well, and will bark at and run away from those who give them rough fare. It is in the value of being born a human being that—and this goes without saying for those who treat us well—if one is kind to those who treat him poorly, even they may change their ways. And even if they do not, he will have the love of the gods and Buddhas, and those who see and hear of his acts will praise him.

If one treats men roughly in this existence, he will be roughly treated by them in the next, for karma is never-ending in all things. And if one would rid himself of bad karma in this round of existence, he should treat well those who are not so kind to him. For if one is dealt with kindly by people, he can rejoice in his previous existence; but if he is handled roughly in this world, his previous existence is a matter for regret.

When one buys something, he should say exactly what he wants at once. If it is too expensive, then he should not buy it. To waste so many words is vulgar, and to buy cheaply would be a crime, for the shopkeeper makes his living by trade.

When one's wife or children are relating some matter to him, he should listen to them with care. If they say something unreasonable, he should consider that to be in the nature of women and children. Moreover, if they speak with reason he should be somewhat impressed and encourage them to speak in such a way hereafter. One should not look down on them because they are women

41

and children. Amaterasu Omikami takes the form of a woman, and the Empress Jingu, as a queen, attacked and subjugated the Korean kingdom of Silla. Again, one should not look down upon children, for the god Hachiman[1] ruled from the time he was a child. One should rely on neither age nor youth. But he who reveres the master and protects the people may be called a sage.

When one loses at gambling, he should take the consequences quickly. When he wins he should not taunt the loser.

One should not dicker over the results of gambling.

When one is associating with prostitutes and dancing girls, he should not consider that, as they are such, he can go to excesses and speak in an overly familiar manner with them. One should act and speak in a simple and ordinary way. Going too far, one may bring shame upon himself.

When one is selecting a partner from a number of prostitutes, he should pick one who is unattractive and whose dress is less comely. A man will lose his heart to an attractive girl, but an unattractive one will have no partner. Moreover, one's heart will not be taken in this way. And as this will be for only one night, one can imagine that the prostitute will be pleased too.

When one is at a drinking party he should always pay attention to and speak with the person at the lowest seat. Even if it is with the same wine that one is drinking, if he will feel sympathy for the man and pour for him, the man will be very pleased. One should be especially sympathetic with men of low positions. In their boundless gratification they will place great importance in one's orders.

In becoming accustomed to riding in a boat, in knowing the particulars of a river, in learning to climb a mountain, in heat and in cold, one should learn all these things with endurance.

One should not talk about the faults of others, even as a joke. For even though one may think of it as a joke, to others it may be embarrassing, and this is a bad mistake. If one would joke, he should joke about things that are a pleasure to others. One should have restraint and deep sympathy in all things.

One should not talk about a woman's faults, no matter how humble of origin she may be. This goes without saying for women of position. One should use discretion in talking about people's good points, and should say nothing about their bad ones. A person who has no judgment in these matters will likely bring shame upon himself. Such things have no merit at all.

One should have insight into this world of dreams that passes in the twinkling of an eye.

By means of an oar, a boat is able to bear out frightening waves, protect itself from rough winds, and cross great seas. As for a man who is born into this world, he may cross it with the help of the gods and Buddhas by means of an upright heart. Relying on an upright heart, when it comes time to take the trip to the Nether World, there should be a path across the Mountain of Death and a bridge across the River Styx. Such a heart would seem to be a jewel for which there is no occasion to put away. One should understand this well.

An upright heart is free of avarice, and a lack of avarice will be an aid in the life to come. One should have insight into this world of dreams that passes in the twinkling of an eye.

Postscript

Although it is certainly shameful of me to go on like this, a man's life has its determined limit, and one cannot know when his end is coming. Moreover, concerning the conditions of facing that moment, there have been men who passed away leaving nothing said, and others who have left this world in the midst of battle. Man's fate is like the dew, and follows the uncertain wind of life and death. Even one's relationship with his child is as uncertain as the simmering of a heat wave. Thus, I have spoken the things that have come to mind without hesitation.

If you[2] would put these things into effect and the results turn out poorly, you should blame your father at that time for having spoken evil. But I feel that putting them into practice would be the highest discharge of one's filial duties. And even if you do not put them into practice, you should pass them on to your descendants until the end of time. For among the descendants to come, if one in the midst of a hundred were to put these into practice, he might wonder if they weren't perhaps something that had been passed down by one of his ancestors.

It is presumptuous for a man's parent to meddle with his children, and you may think that what I am about to say is exactly that, but I hope that you will sit peacefully with two or three of your children and read this to them. You should not think that what has been said here is simply something handed down to you from your father. You should understand that these are precepts for men in ages to come.

Again, as I feel unusually shameful about these things, do not let them out to other people.

See this as a memento
Of a person of the past,
And with one breath intone:
Namu Amida Butsu.[3]

Notes

[1] One of the most important gods in the Shinto pantheon, and in this case indicating the 15th emperor of Japan, Ojin.

[2] Hojo wrote this to his son, Nagatoki, but the whole was for all the members of Hojo's clan.

[3] "Hail to the Buddha Amitabha," would be a close translation. It refers to the Buddha who has the power to save all beings, and the invocation is spoken at the hour of death to open the entrance to Paradise. It is repeated constantly by members of the Pure Land sect of Buddhism.

THE CHIKUBASHO

"In this uncertain world, ours should be the path of discipline."

THE CHIKUBASHO

Shiba Yoshimasa
(1350-1410 A.D.)

Shiba Yoshimasa was a warrior leader during the Namboku and Muromachi Periods, and was known as an administrator, general and poet. The Shiba, a branch family of the Ashikaga, joined the Hatakeyama and Hosokawa to make up the three families whose members held the office kanrei (chief administrator), and Shiba held this position under Ashikaga shoguns Yoshiakira, Yoshimitsu and Yoshimochi. His career was spotted, much like those of other great men of this period. At the age of 12 he was appointed to the major office of Shitsuji, only to be discharged four years later when his father, Shiba Takatsune, offended a group of warrior-monks and was driven from Kyoto. In 1378, however, when a group of daimyo drove the Kanrei Hosokawa Yoriyuki from power, Shiba took his place in the office for the next 12 years, strengthening the bakufu and renewing trade with Ming China. In 1391 the situation was once again reversed, bringing the return of Hosokawa. Finally, at the age of 60, he held the office of kanrei for the last few months prior to his death.

Shiba Yoshimasa lived during a time marked by both political reverses and great cultural advances, and it is cultural gains by the warrior class that are so evident in the Chikubasho, *a document he wrote at the age of 33 for the young men of his clan. A short list of precepts written in a classical Japanese style, the* Chikubasho *displays both the ethical morality of the warrior and the tasteful lifestyle of the aristocracy. Its tone is a combination of a manly Confucian approach reflecting honesty and fairness, and a Buddhist sympathy for others. One is admonished to use his head well and be disciplined, for a man is old before he knows it; and unless he enters into things, his accomplishments will be few. Very striking is Shiba's emphasis on the arts and their effect on the reputation of the individual and of the clan. He considered these social graces as well, and in this document we can see how close the upper echelons of the warrior class moved toward the ideals of the nobility without moving away from their own.*

The Chikubasho

In all things there is a comprehensive attitude that is important to have, but generally, there are few men of these times who have thought this through to a clear understanding.

First, a man whose profession is the use of arms should think and then act upon not only his own fame, but also that of his descendants. He should not scandalize his name forever by holding his one and only life too dear. On the other hand, in the light of this, to consider this life that is given to us only once as nothing more than dust and ashes, and lose it at a time when one should not, would be to gain a reputation that is not worth mentioning. One's main purpose in throwing away his life is to do so either for the sake of the Emperor or in some great undertaking of a military general. It is that exactly that will be the great fame of one's descendants.

To be involved in some ephemeral quarrel will demonstrate the indiscretion of one's house and will not add to one's fame, regardless of being in the right or in the wrong.

A warrior generally should not be unmindful and lax, but rather should think everything over ahead of time. Watanabe no Tsuna instructed Urabe no Suetake[1] that his everyday mind should be like that of a coward, which meant that one should be prepared beforehand for the final great event.

Many men feel that they should act according to the time or just according to the moment they are facing, and thus are in confusion when something goes beyond this and some difficulty instantaneously arises. It is a matter of regret to let the moment when one should die pass by. It has been said to the effect that the preparedness of the warrior and that of the monk are the same. In all matters it is a regrettable thing not to pacify one's mind.

Men with sharpness of mind are to be found only among those with a penchant for thought.

A person's character and depth of mind may be seen by his behavior. Thus, one should understand that even the fences and walls have eyes, and not become negligent even when alone.

Much more so for behavior in the midst of people, one should not take a single step in vain, or speak a word in a way that others may speak of him as shallow.

Many men feel that they should act according to the time or the moment they are facing, and thus are in confusion when something goes beyond this and some difficulty arises.

Moreover, even people who like refinement and elegance in their lives should add these qualities to themselves after making their hearts upright and true. When there is no truth even in relations between men and women, without a refined sincerity there will be little to deeply move the heart.

One will only go against the teachings of his parents if he thinks first of his own situation and regards their advice as troublesome. Even if one's parents are lacking in wisdom, if one will follow their precepts he will first of all likely not be turning his back on the Way of Heaven. More than this, in eight or nine times out of ten, parents' words will be in accord with the reasoning of their child. Thus, one's own mistakes may be reflected upon.

The words of one's parents that in the past one found vexing or rejected in principle are all important. Rather than imitating the good in others, one should imitate his own faulty parents. This in itself will carry on the clan traditions and provide for one's descendants.

That the gods and Buddhas should be revered is likely known by anyone who is a man, and does not warrant being mentioned anew. But in this connection there is a small matter that should be understood.

The Buddha appeared and the gods manifested themselves in this world entirely for its sake and for the sake of those living in it. Thus, it was not to injure man, but to make his heart pure, to make correct his sense of humanity, justice, propriety, wisdom and faithfulness, and to make clear the foundation of his life. Yet, was there something further expressed in their appearances?

Those who do not understand this basic point confess their belief in the Buddhas but bring trouble to the people, taking their belongings, and building temples or monasteries. Or, declaring their respect for the gods, they deprive men of their lands only to perform shrine services. One should know that such acts are a sacrilege to both the gods and Buddhas.

Even though one has never offered a single service to the Buddha or made a pilgrimage to a shrine, if his heart is upright and full of compassion, neither the gods, nor Buddhas will look at him amiss. The great god of Ise, the Bodhisattva Hachiman, and the god of Kitano in particular are likely to reside in the heads of those who are gentle and pure.

Again, there are men who pray at the shrines only when they themselves are in distress. This is a sad situation, indeed. The desire of the gods and Buddhas is nothing other than that we pray for happiness in the world to come, and in such there is effect. Yet it is taught that even that does not approach directly the road to Truth.

There are men who believe that when one is serving the lord, he first receives the lord's favor and only then makes endeavors in loyalty and his duties. They have understood the matter in reverse. Being able to live in this world is from the beginning by the grace of one's lord. It is a sad thing for men to forget this and, while setting their ambitions yet higher, envy their masters and the world at large.

It is a regrettable and selfish thing for a man who should be a benefit to the world to deprecate his position and feel that all is well as long as he is at peace. Receiving human life, one should vow to transcend the rest of mankind and be of aid to men, exhausting his mind for the sake of others, and making this his satisfaction to the end of time. The Bodhisattvas acted on this account alone, and should a common man live being equal to their vow, would there be any satisfaction parallel to this?

The man whose profession is arms should calm his mind and look into the depths of others. Doing so is likely the best of the martial arts.

When a man has ability in the arts, the depth of his heart can be conjectured and the mind of his clan surmised. This world values reputation alone and, as a man will gain fame in the arts, too, he should put his mind to them, regardless of his lack of skill. To the extent that a man studies with some interest, though he may be lacking in talent, if he will put out effort he will not be ashamed in front of others. It is only rarely that a thing is done well, but with persistence one should be able to join others in these pursuits and this should be considered valuable. No matter how noble a family one may be born into or how good-looking he may be, when people are picking up manuscripts, for the recitation of chants, thinking over the rhymes in making poetry, or tuning up their instruments, how deplorable it must be to be among people reciting linked verse and to have to make some excuse for one's inability, or to sit chin in hands while others are playing music together, or to be even unable to join in the beginning of a game of football. It is needless to say that this is also true when one has received a well-written letter from a young friend and, in making a reply has to use the unsatisfactory means of dictating the letter to someone else more able. How much more so embarrassing when one must ask someone to write a letter for him to a young lady, and this fact, which should be kept hidden,

becomes known. To not know how to join in even with such pas-
time games as *go, shogi,* or *sugoroku*[2] when others are gathered
together is awkward indeed. That one should be well practiced in
such archery sports as *mato, kasagake,* and *inu-oumono,* goes without saying and should be an understood matter.

A man with intelligence and a firm heart will be able to put
others to use. People's ways are variant, and to use a man to whom
one has taken a liking for all things—for example, to use a military
man for literary matters, or a man untalented in speech as a messenger, or a slow-thinking man in a place where a quick wit is
necessary—may bring about failure and even cause a man's life to
be ruined. A man should be put to use in the line with which he
seems most familiar.

When men are put to use in the same way that curved wood is
used for the wheel and straight wood for the shaft, there will be
no one without value.

Thus, won't there even be use for a man, according to the matter at hand, for whom one does not particularly care? What will it
value a man to not put another to use on the grounds of dislike for
him? It is truly as stated above, that a man lacking sincerity in his
heart is likely to gain no merit in anything. The saying that all
abilities come from the heart applies to such situations.

Particularly the man whose profession is arms should calm his
mind and look into the depths of others. Doing so is likely the
best of the martial arts.

It is fairly certain that most ordinary men have picked up the
Genji Monogatari and Sei Shonagon's *Makura Soshi* and read
through them any number of times. There is nothing like these
books for the instruction of man's behavior and the baring of the
quality of his heart. Reading them, one will naturally be able to
recognize a man with soul.

Surely one should not act inconsiderately to another's distress,
entertain a deep craving for things, or make worthless fellows
one's friends. It is in the nature of man that the good is difficult to
learn while the bad is easily taken to, and thus one naturally
becomes gradually like those with whom he is familiar. I myself
have realized this deeply. That I have practiced the art of calligraphy stems from the fact that I once noted with embarrassment

how well a certain lady wrote her characters. That along with everyone else I began studying *waka*, getting my name mentioned in the poetry collection, *Shingoshui Wakashu*,[3] and that I became involved with writing linked verse all comes from the fact that I competed with my young friends, at first with egotism and later with thought to reputation. Thus, naturally and with the passage of time, my heart drew close to this subject and I have mixed with those who are likewise inclined.

When men become old they are treated with aversion by others, and it is difficult to participate in society. If, then, one is not connected with any arts at all, neither will his existence be recognized by others, nor will he have anything with which to soothe his own mind.

As for playing football, when I was young I was urged to fill in because of a lack of players, and, to the extent that I associated without being ashamed with those fellows, in the end the result was that, although not so dashing, I was able to distinguish men of the art, good and bad technique, and calmness of mind. Thus, I was brought to shame by no one, regardless of their skill.

As for the study of music, that, too, was stressed by my parents, and as an aid in the study of the three basic lute melodies I was taught the use of the drum from before the time I can remember. This study was cut off half way due to work and lack of time. My intentions, then, were in vain, for after that I was no longer able to associate with men who studied such things. This is regrettable.

Concerning this matter, too, one's art is affected by his friends. The men and women of both past and present who have gained names in the world of the arts have done so on no special accounts. They simply imbued their minds with the moon and flowers, looked through to the transcience of this world, made their hearts tender, knew the *aware*[4] of things, and purified their intentions. Thus they gained fame in the Way of the Arts by their gentleness and their superlative artistic sense and ability.

When one thinks over these matters, it would seem that in today's world we lack such cultivated people. While yet in the vigor of youth, men put their pride in a vaguely pleasing appearance; thinking only of themselves and their desires, they neither discipline their minds nor wish to become more refined. When meeting with those who see straight through to the heart, will not such

men be quickly scorned? When one thinks about such unculti-
vated men growing old, they seem no different than again foxes
and badgers. And what will be done then?

> *"Cherry blossoms that fall in confusion,*
> *Conceal the road that is travelled*
> *By my approaching old age."*
>
> Ariwara no Narihira

> *"Only awaiting my end,*
> *Will it be today or tomorrow?*
> *Kai's⁵ waterfall of tears or my own.*
> *Which sheds the more?"*
>
> Ariwara no Yukihira

> *"Then I'll climb Mirror Mountain and have a look!*
> *This body passed by with so many years,*
> *Won't it look old?"*
>
> Otomo no Kuronushi

> *"Think of it: eighty years have drawn to a close.*
> *How could it be?*
> *Ah, the transience of things!"*
>
> The daughter of Ki no Mitsukiyo

When we recall that these poems were recited and loved in the
resplendent past, we hear in them both pathos and gentility.

When a man puts all his stock in youth, what will be his
thoughts when old age has come? Though one's span seems only a
dream or apparition, his name may last to the end of time. But unless as a famous Buddhist priest, sage, or saint, or again as a man of
refinement, who will be known for long in the generations to
come? Though it is said that men are made of neither wood nor
stone, are not those who spend their lives for naught no different
than the rotting trees in the shadow of the valley?

One should use prudence in this matter.

There is nothing more base than for a man to lose his temper
too often. No matter how angry one becomes, his first thought
should be to pacify his mind and come to a clear understanding of
the situation at hand. Then, if he is in the right, to become angry
is correct.

Becoming angry simply on account of one's own bias is unreasonable, and one will not be held in respect. Thus, though one may become more and more angry, there will be no result. It is Reason alone by which people feel humbled and for which they feel respect. Simply, when one becomes angry, he should repeatedly calm his mind and think the matter over. It is a good thing not to be ashamed of correcting one's mistakes. To take something oneself has done to heart and push it through, regardless of its good or evil, is a disaster of the first order.

It should also be said that it is not good for others and does harm to oneself to simply remain tranquil and speaking like a three-year-old child, never becoming angry, bearing rancor, or deploring matters when one should. This goes also for letting situations pass by when one should definitely speak his mind to another, in the end becoming known by all as overly accommodating. It is a good thing to keep one's mind tranquil, yet to speak what one should when there is a situation that should be reprimanded, and thus not become known as completely mindless.

Long ago, when all men were good-natured, we could call such men either good or bad. But nowadays, as people either look down on others or carry only evil in their hearts, they distain those who are only gentle and correct.

The Buddhists who take the Way of Selflessness seem to be lacking both eye and mind, but when they talk as three-year-old children it is yet another thing.

Moreover, a fool who sits speechless, unable to descriminate the good from the bad, would surely not be called a good man. Such things should be thought over well.

The priests that practice *zazen* were not born clever, but became enlightened to all things by pacifying their minds. Scholars, too, to the extent that they study with great respect to what is before them and pacify their minds, become naturally clever about other matters, too.

Whether a man becomes good or bad, clever or thickwitted, is simply a matter of the way he uses his mind. A man's peak years do not number over ten. During that time a man should put out effort for at least something. From the time one is ten to the time he is 14 or 15, he is interested in nothing truly. Becoming 14 or 15 he is still slow and unappreciative of anything, and even considerable discipline at this time will not come up to one's expecta-

tions. From the time one is 18 or 19 to the time he is 30, his mind
has come to order, and he arrives at the fountainhead of interest;
yet this period does not go beyond 12 or 13 years.

In this uncertain world, ours should be the path of discipline.

It is the nature of this world we live in that, of our desires, not
one out of ten comes out the way we would like. It is doubtful
that even the Emperor has things the way he would like them to
be. In spite of that, for one to persist willfully in affairs that have
not gone according to his heart's desire, will, in the end, be inviting the admonishment of Heaven. No man should think of getting
satisfaction today concerning something he felt chagrined by yesterday, or gaining this year an ambition that was frustrated the
year before.

---

*It is the nature of this world we live in that, of our desires, not
one out of ten comes out the way we would like.*

If we *do* act in this vein, the desires of our hearts will rise up
one after another like dust in the wind, and our affairs will be af-
flicted by the same. As much as possible, it is better to forget such
aspirations, for he who would tender rancor in his heart is a mor-
tifyingly perverse man. Such a wretch is despised in both the secular and Buddhist worlds alike. Any man who has some egotistical
attachment that he will not forget will surely be narrow-minded
and effeminate. In sweeping these things aside and not letting
them stay in one's heart, other and better thoughts will arise.

One should take great care to put man first in all things, and to
ridicule no one.

Even when in a battle that is beyond one's means to win, one
should lift up his heart and be resolved that no one will surpass
him in firmness. He should think to be another's strength and a
man to be relied upon.

No matter how friendly a man may be with one, he should not
be asked about battles if he is born a coward.

One should not consider evading an impending battle just because of its enormity. Nor should one advocate a battle that
should not be fought on account of its being unexacting.

For battles generally, when they are likely to be unexacting, one should put others to the fore. But for situations of crisis, even if it be a hundred times, one should be of the mind to take action himself. Unfair behavior is extraordinarily bad in battle.

Such matters are only what this foolish man has come to know, and, entirely from a parent's excess of compassion I write them down for my possibly even more foolish descendants.

To the best of your abilities, cultivate and take care of yourselves. You should think over all things in depth.

February 9th, 1383,
the third year of Eitoku[6]

Notes

[1] Two retainers of Minamoto no Yorimitsu (944-1021), famous, along with their master, for various military feats.

[2] *Go, shogi, sugoroku:* types of board games; *mato:* shooting at a fixed target from a galloping horse; *kasagake:* shooting at a sort of reed rainhat with a protruding top, also on horseback; *inu-oumono:* shooting at dogs from horseback with harmless, whistling arrows.

[3] An Imperial anthology completed in 1384, and consisting of 1,554 verses. In the original text it is called *The Anthology of Two Generations*, as the editorship was passed from one Fujiwara upon his death to another.

[4] Once an expletive used when something is keenly felt, it now indicates the quality itself of that feeling. It is often translated as "pathos" or "moving."

[5] A province in Eastern Japan.

[6] A period name; up until 1868 emperors would change the name of the "period" a number of times during their reign depending on the occurrence of natural disasters or other important events.

THE REGULATIONS OF
IMAGAWA RYOSHUN

"Just as water will conform to the shape of the vessel that contains it, so will a man follow the good and evil of his companions."

THE REGULATIONS OF IMAGAWA RYOSHUN

Imagawa Sadayo
(1325-1420 A.D.)

Imagawa Sadayo was one of the most remarkable men of his age. He ranked as a leading general and strategist along with Kusunoki and Kitabatake, and as a poet and scholar became a prominent figure in the Court-dominated literary world, composing both historical works and poetry.

The Imagawa were a cadet family of the Ashikaga, taking their name from their manor at Imagawa in Mikawa Province. Imagawa's father had supported the Shogun Takauji and had been rewarded with the governorship of Suruga Province. Here the clan settled and in time formed marriage ties with the Court nobility.

Imagawa's military career began with the dispute of the Northern and Southern Courts. He chose to back the Northern Court and by 1361 had defeated Hosokawa Kiyouji at the fighting in Yoshino. Returning to Kyoto, he shaved his head and entered religion, taking the name of Ryoshun. By 1370, the bakufu had lost control of most of the island of Kyushu and sent Ryoshun to serve as military governor to pacify the area. To this task he devoted the next decade of his life, at the same time continuing his literary interests and contacts with his teacher, Nijo Yoshimoto.

In 1395 it was suggested to the Shogun Yoshimitsu that Ryoshun was by far too powerful and held rebellious intentions. Thus he was recalled to his governorship in Suruga where he devoted most of his remaining years to literature and poetry.

Ryoshun was the author of a number of literary works and documents, among them the Michiyukiburi, *a travel diary including some of his own poetry; the* Nan Taiheiki, *an historical work; and the present text, the* Regulations, *written in 1412 for his younger brother, Tadaaki. Also called the* Imagawa Wall Inscriptions, *the* Regulations *has been respected and studied as a text on proper morality up until WWII, and used during the Edo period as a basic text in temple schools. Written in* kanbun, *it sets down the classic view that a warrior must be a man of both military skill and of letters—that lacking one, he will lack both. As a Buddhist, Ryoshun proscribed the wanton taking of life, but as a member of the warrior class, he held great respect for his profession. As a Confucian, he cited the Chinese Classics and demanded respect for one's family, as well as stressing the concept of loyalty and duty to one's master. In him we see the ideal of the warrior at its most balanced stage.*

The Regulations of Imagawa Ryoshun

Without knowledge of Learning, one will ultimately have no military victories.

Cormorant fishing and falconing are pleasures that uselessly destroy life. They are forbidden.

It is forbidden to pass the death sentence on a man who has committed a minor crime without full investigation.

It is forbidden to use favoritism and excuse a man who has committed a major crime.

It is forbidden to bring about one's own excessive prosperity by means of exploiting the people and causing the destruction of shrines.

It is forbidden to tear down one's ancestors' family temples and pagodas, thereby embellishing one's own domicile.

It is forbidden to forget the great debt of kindness one owes to his master and ancestors and thereby make light of the virtues of loyalty and filial piety.

It is forbidden that one should, acting disrespective of the Way of Heaven, attach little importance to his duties to his master and be overly attentive to his own business.

It is forbidden to be indiscriminate of one's retainers' good or evil actions and to distribute unjust rewards and punishments.

Be mindful of the fact that, as you know the works of your own retainers, the master knows yours in the same way.

It is forbidden to disrupt the relationships of other people, and to make others' anguish your own pleasure.

It is forbidden to put others' profit at a loss and, recklessly embracing one's own ambition, increase one's own power.

It is forbidden to be disregardful of one's own financial status, and to live either too far above or below it.

It is forbidden to have contempt for wise retainers and prefer flatterers, and to have one's actions be influenced by these conditions.

One should not be envious of someone who has prospered by unjust deeds. Nor should he disdain someone who has fallen while adhering to the path of righteousness.

It is forbidden to be given up to drinking and carousing and, in gambling and the like, to forget one's family duties.

It is forbidden to be prideful of one's own cleverness, and to ridicule others about everything.

When a person comes to one's home, it is forbidden to feign illness and thus avoid meeting him.

It is forbidden to enjoy only one's own tranquility, and to retire a man without adding to him some stipend.

It is forbidden to be excessive in one's own clothing and armor, while his retainers go about shabbily.

One should be highly reverential of Buddhist priests, and treat them with correct manners.

Regardless of a person's high or low position, it is forbidden to disregard the law of karma, and to simply live in ease.

It is forbidden to erect barriers within one's own domain and thus cause distress to travelers both coming and going.

The above articles should be kept in mind at all times.

Postscript

It is natural that training in the martial arts is the Way of the Warrior, but it is most important to put them into actual practice. First, it is clearly written in the Four Books and the Five Classics[1] as well as in the military writings that in protecting the country, if one is ignorant of Learning he will be unable to govern. From the time one is young, he should associate with companions who are upright, and not even temporarily be taken in by friends of low character. Just as water will conform to the shape of the vessel that contains it, so will a man follow the good and evil of his companions. This is so true. Therefore it is said that the master who governs his domain well loves wise retainers, while the man who exploits the people loves flatterers. This means that if one would know the heart of the master, he should look to the companions whom the master loves. One should truly take this to heart. To prefer friends who are superior to him, and to avoid those who are his inferiors, is the wisdom of the good man. How-

ever, considering this to be true, it will not do to be overly fastidi-
ous in one's choice of people. This is simply saying that one
should not love those who are evil. This is not limited to the man
who governs the country, for without the love and respect of the
masses, all matters are difficult to achieve.

First of all, a samurai who dislikes battle and who has not put
his heart in the right place even though he has been born in the
house of the warrior, should not be reckoned among one's retainers. Many famous generals have made this admonition. Next, if
one would wonder about the good and evil of his own heart, he
may think of himself as good if many people of both high and low
positions gather at his door. And, even if one invites many people,
and still they neglect him and he has no comrades, he should think
of his own conduct as being incorrect.

Yet, I suppose there are two ways of having the gate crowded
with callers. There are also occasions when the people are fearful
of the master's iniquity, are exploited by the high-handedness of
his retainers and oppressed by the plots of his companions, and
will gather at the gates of the authorities complaining of their af-
flictions with explanations of their distress. One should be able to
discern such situations well and to correct the arbitrariness of his
retainers. He should entrust himself to the wise sayings of the ancients and follow the conditions of the law.

A man who is said to be a master should, in the same way that
the sun and moon shine on the grass and trees all over the land,
ponder day and night with a heart of compassion into the matters
of rewards and punishments for his vassals both near and far, and
even to those officials separated from him by mountains and sea;
and he should use those men according to their talents. It is possible that there are many cases of men becoming leaders of samurai, and yet being negligent and lacking wisdom and ability, and
thus incurring the criticism of men both high and low. Just as the
Buddha preached the various laws in order to save all living beings,[2] one must rack one's brains and never depart from the Ways
of both Warrior and Scholar. In governing the country it is dangerous to lack even one of the virtues of humanity, righteousness,
etiquette, and wisdom. In adhering to correct government, there
will be no rancor from the people when crimes are punished. But
when the government makes its stand in unrighteousness and the
death penalty is passed, there will be deep lamenting. And in such

a case there will be no escaping the retribution of karma.

There is a primary need to distinguish loyalty from disloyalty and to establish rewards and punishments. It is meaningless to divide up the administration of the domain if one's vassals commit useless acts in their own interests, have no ability in the martial arts, and do not sustain their underlings. And though one can say that the treatment of his vassals in the division of the fiefs has not differed since the time of his ancestors, differences in conduct and authority are dependent on the frame of mind of the present master.

Being born into a family that has from the beginning earnestly known the Way of Battle, it is truly regrettable to wastefully tamper with the domain, support no soldiers, and receive the scorn of all.

Thus is the above written.

in the 19th year of Oei (1412)

Notes

[1] The basic Confucian texts. The Four Books are the *Analects*, the *Great Learning*, the *Doctrine of the Mean* and the *Book of Mencius*. The Five Classics are the *Odes*, the *Book of History*, the *Book of Rites*, the *Book of Changes* and the *Book of Spring and Autumn Annals*.

[2] According to Mahayana Buddhism, the Buddha Shakamuni preached in various ways so that sentient beings of all levels would be able to understand and reach Nirvana.

THE SEVENTEEN ARTICLES
OF ASAKURA TOSHIKAGE

"Even if one has learned all the sayings of the sages and saints, he should not insist on them obstinately."

THE SEVENTEEN ARTICLES
OF ASAKURA TOSHIKAGE

Asakura Toshikage
(1428-1481 A.D.)

The Asakura, claiming descent from several emperors, were established in the province of Echizen as hereditary vassals of the Shiba clan, and were a powerful force both militarily and economically from the mid-15th century until their final destruction by the forces of Oda Nobunga in 1573.

Asakura Toshikage was recognized for his abilities from his youth, and in 1453 was charged by the bakufu to settle a succession feud between two branches of the Shiba. Using this as an'opportunity for greater things, he began a career of expropriating portions of manors held in Echizen by both religious institutions and the nobility. The Shiba family's real power began to fade rapidly, and by the end of 1471 Asakura was awarded with the governorship of Echizen, an office traditionally held by the Shiba. He then built a castle at Ichijogatani, and the province prospered economically and culturally for nearly 100 years. Ichijogatani became a thriving mercantile center until its destruction in the wars with Oda Nobunaga.

Asakura is considered to have been ruthless and typical of the
gekokujo *daimyo, those lower class warriors who overthrew the*
upper class nobility. He was certainly very realistic and scornful of
superstition. The Seventeen Articles, *written in a heavily Sinicized*
style, were possibly compiled after his death, but are reputed to
reflect his ideas and temperament well. They indicate a sharp prac-
ticality and rationalism, and there is very little of the religious
about him. The choice of the number 17 is reminiscent of the
17-article constitution of Shotoku Taishi written in the seventh
century, and may hint at Asakura's aspirations for his clan and
possibly his own self-image in history.

The Seventeen Articles of Asakura Toshikage

In the fief of the Asakura, one should not determine hereditary
chief retainers. A man should be assigned according to his ability
and loyalty.

One should not entrust a position and land to a man who has no
talent, even if his family has held such for generations.

One should place spies in fiefs both near and far, even in times
of peace, and should constantly inquire into their circumstances.

One should not be overly fond of famous swords and daggers.
For even if one has a sword valued at 10,000 cash, he will not
overcome 100 men carrying spears valued at 100 cash. Therefore,
if one has 10,000 cash and buys 100 spears, having 100 men to
carry them he should be able to protect an entire flank.

One should not be fond of creating a spectacle by periodically
inviting actors from the four schools of Sarugaku[1] to come from
Kyoto. With the expense that would involve, if he would have a
Sarugaku actor of talent from our own fief go to learn in the
capital, he would be able to have enjoyment thereafter.

It is prohibited to perform Noh within the castle grounds at
night.

One should not, saying that is for the use of a samurai, send messengers to the Date[2] or Shirakawa in search of good horses or hawks. It is different, however, if one receives a gift from another place; but that, too, should be sent to another clan within three years. If one retains something for a long time, it will inevitably bring regret.

If a man who serves indolently and a man who serves well are treated in the same way, the man who serves well may begin to wonder why he does so.

Beginning with the immediate members of the Asakura family, all should wear clothing made of cotton at the New Year's first attendance. Likewise, all should be made to wear the family crest. If one thinks that since he has the resources he can dress in fancy attire, the lower ranks of samurai will feel it difficult to appear in a place where such showy costumes are congregated, will feign illness and put in no appearance for a year; and if they will not come for two years, the number of men serving the Asakura will decline.

Among the men serving our clan, if there are some without talent or ability, they should be treated with special charity because of the strength of their determination. Moreover, though it is said that a man is a coward, if his looks and demeanor are exceptional, he should not simply be regarded as a coward. He can be put to use as an attendant or messenger, and should not be cast off to no purpose. However, a man who is lacking in both determination and appearance will amount to absolutely nothing, regardless of the care taken for him.

If a man who serves indolently and a man who serves well are treated in the same way, the man who serves well may begin to wonder why he does so.

Except in cases of extreme difficulty, one should not allow *ronin*[3] from other provinces to act as one's personal scribe.

Among both priests and commoners, if there is a man with some talent or ability, he should not be allowed to leave to some other clan. A man who depends solely on his own ability and serves indolently, however, is worthless.

When there is a battle that can be won or a castle that can be taken, to concern oneself with the fortuitous day or direction[4] and let time pass is extremely regrettable. There will be little value in sending a ship out in a storm, or having a single man face great numbers even if the day is propitious. For even though the day and place be "unlucky," if one will attain the minute details of the situation, prepare his attack in secret, adapt to the circumstances, and make strategy his foundation, the victory will surely be his.

Three times a year one should have an able and honest retainer go around the province, listen to the opinions of the four classes of people,[5] and devise some policy in regard to those opinions. Moreover, the master should also change his appearance a bit and make such an inspection for himself.

It should be strictly forbidden to construct in our province any castle other than the one (Ichijogatani) held by the Asakura family. All men of high rank should be constantly maintained at Ichijogatani, and only their representatives and underlings should be placed in their home areas.

When passing by shrines and temples or through village streets, from time to time one should rein in his horse and praise places of beauty or lament for those that have gone to ruin. If he will do so, the joy of the common people at having been spoken to by the master will know no bounds, and they are likely to quickly repair places in need and to be all the more scrupulous in places of perfection. Thus, encouraging the people without taking great efforts will be chiefly a matter of the single-mindedness of the master.

When one is giving direct audience to various reports, he should not allow the least bit of distortion in terms of their truth or falsehood. If he hears that an official has put his own profit to the fore, he should be strictly given the proper punishment.

One should keep the above items well in mind, exert himself in them day and night, and pass them down to descendant after descendant. In all things, if one is firm from within there will be no evil men to cause disturbances from without.

Postscript

When various reports are being given, one should not allow the least bit of distortion in terms of their truth or falsehood. If one hears that an official has put his own profit to the fore, he should be strictly ordered to the proper punishment. In all things, if one will scrutinize the interior and take the proper steps for it, there will be no evil men entering from without. For other clans will come to meddle if one's own slipshod conditions are known.

According to a certain priest, a master of men should be like Fudo-o-myo[6] and Aizen-o-myo;[7] the reason being that Fudo-o-myo carries the sword and Aizen-o-myo carries the bow and arrow, not to strike at man, but solely for the subjugation of evil, for they are both gods of deep inner compassion.

Moreover, a lord of men will praise the good and punish the evil, and should judge correctly between truth and falsehood, and good and bad. Such a thing can be called the "taking of life with compassion."

Even if one has learned all the sayings of the sages and saints, he should not insist on them obstinately. In the *Analects* of Confucius it is said, "If a gentleman is not solemn, he will have no dignity." But it would be a mistake to understand this as meaning that one should be solemn all the time. It is necessary to be solemn or light-hearted according to the occasion.

There will be no value in these articles if they are simply thought over casually. After I, a man of little rank, unexpectedly took control of the province, I have put forth great effort both day and night, at one time gathered together famous men of all kinds, listened carefully to what they had to say, and have continued in such a way up until this time. If one will be sufficiently prudent and have his descendants keep the articles written in this book and think of them as the teachings of Marishiten[8] or Hachiman,[9] the name of the Asakura should continue happily. But in the distant future, if our descendants act only with self-interest, it will certainly be a matter of regret.

Imagawa Ryoshun's verse:

When a parent thinks of his child
With a heart of sincerity,
How will he teach him
Without vacillation and doubt?[10]

Notes

[1] Noh Drama. The four schools of Noh at the time were the Kanze, Hosho, Konparu and Kongo.

[2] A powerful family that controlled the area of Mutsu, in the northeast of Japan, and who were apparently famous for raising such animals.

[3] A warrior who is not in the service of a master, either due to the death of his master or by being expelled from service.

[4] This and the following allusions to "lucky" and "unlucky" days and locations have to do with the Oriental concern for a proper understanding of cosmology and the individual's harmony with it. This belief probably had its origin in the early Chinese yin-yang philosophy and is not entirely ignored today throughout the Oriental world.

[5] Samurai, farmers, artisans and merchants.

[6] A Buddhist diety represented with a fearsome appearance, clutching a sword in one hand and a cord in the other to strike down and bind the spirits of evil.

[7] A Buddhist goddess of love, also fearsome and represented with three eyes and six arms. She, too, carries weapons and is colored red.

[8] A Buddhist diety who is a protector of warriors.

[9] A high-ranking Buddhist diety also connected with the Shinto pantheon and the early Emperor Ojin. Hachiman is also associated with war.

[10] Asakura was not unlettered, and Ryoshun was well known as a literary person. This reinforces the idea that samurai were men of letters as well as warriors.

THE TWENTY-ONE
PRECEPTS OF HOJO SOUN

"One should always be genteel in his speaking. A man shows his inmost self by a single word."

THE TWENTY-ONE PRECEPTS OF HOJO SOUN

Hojo Nagauji
(1432-1519 A.D.)

Hojo Nagauji was a general of the late Muromachi Period who, through marriage and a succession of political maneuvers, became master of the Suruga, Izu and Sagami Provinces. His origins are obscure, but he may have been connected with the Heiji of Ise, and first went by the name of Ise Skinkuro. Later he married off his son, Ujitsuna, to a descendant of the ancient Hojo family and took their name for his own, supposedly for the prestige it would render and possibly to indicate his own political intentions. His line is called the Go-Hojo, or the Later Hojo.

Around 1475 Hojo Nagauji came to Suruga and attached himself to the Imagawa clan, later taking advantage of a succession problem within that clan to become master of the province. In 1491, under similar circumstances, he was able to add Izu to his domains; and finally in 1495, under the pretense of hunting for deer, he marched into Sagami, taking the castle town of Odawara. From this point, Nagauji extended his attacks and eventually his domains northward, fighting successively with the Uesugi and other neighboring clans. At Odawara he built one of the first great castle towns in Japan, attracting many samurai from other fiefs by its general prosperity and peace. In his later years he became a priest, taking the name Soun.

Like Asakura Toshikage, Hojo Soun has not received great praise from historians due to his somewhat cunning and ruthless methods in extending his domains. Yet he was admired by other daimyo as a good general and administrator. In addition to attracting more samurai to Odawara, he cut crop taxes from one-half to two-fifths of the harvest, and generally looked out for the welfare of his people.

The Twenty-One Precepts *were written some time after Hojo Soun had become a priest, and reflect the fullness of his own experiences. The articles are basically rules for the daily life of the common warrior, and show his familiarity and sympathy for those in the lower echelons. The subject matter ranges from encouraging the study of poetry and horsemanship and the avoidance of games like chess and* go, *to advice on how to keep one's house in better order and well-protected. There is a strong tone of self-reliance throughout, reflecting Hojo Soun's unsparingly meticulous character and his own rise to power.*

The Twenty-One Precepts of Hojo Soun

Above all, believe in the gods and Buddhas.

In the morning, rise as early as possible. Rising late, one will be negligent as a servant and a hinderance to both the master's and one's own business; and, in the end, one will be forsaken by the master. Great prudence should be taken in this matter.

One should be soundly asleep at night before eight o'clock, for thieves are most likely to break in between midnight and two in the morning. Having useless long conversation at night, one will be asleep between 12 and two, his money will be taken, and damage will be done. This will not be good for one's reputation.

One should put away the firewood and lamp oil that would be uselessly burned away during the night, and at four in the morning rise and do his ablutions and devotions, dress oneself properly, explain the day's labors to his wife and retainers, and go to attend his work before six o'clock. According to an old proverb, one should retire by midnight and rise by four in the morning, but this is up to the individual. Rising by four o'clock would be beneficial for anyone, however. Staying in bed until eight or ten in the morning, one will complete neither his work for the master nor his own private business, and the opportunity of the day will be wasted for no reason at all.

Before washing one's face and hands in the morning, one should first check the lavatory, the stables, and outside the gate; instruct the appropriate people concerning the places needing cleaning, and then quickly wash himself.

One should not assume that water is plentiful, and carelessly wash his mouth out and throw it away. Furthermore, one should do this quietly and not assume that, as he is in his own home, he can go about gargling and spitting loudly, for this is acting without reserve toward others and is unpleasant to hear. There is a saying that goes, "Walk stealthily where still under the arch of heaven."[1]

Consider that which exists to exist and that which does not exist to not exist, and recognize things just as they are. With such a frame of mind, one will have divine protection even though he does not pray.

To worship the gods and Buddhas is the correct conduct for a man. It can be said that one will be in conformity with the feelings of the gods and Buddhas if he will simply make his heart straightforward and calm, respect honestly and wholeheartedly those above him and have pity on those below, consider that which exists to exist and that which does not exist to not exist, and recognize things just as they are. With such a frame of mind, one will have divine protection even though he does not pray. But if his mind is not straight, he had best be prudent lest it be said that he has been abandoned by Heaven, prayerful or not.

It will not do to think that one must have swords and clothing as fine as everyone else's. It is sufficient to intend not to be unsightly. Borrowing and seeking after things one doesn't have, and piling up debts, one will be scorned by others.

Even when one is thinking of staying home all day due to illness or private business, he should quickly arrange his hair. This goes without saying when he is going out to his responsibilities. To expose people to one's sloppy appearance is both impolite and incompetent. If a person himself is negligent concerning these matters, his retainers, too, are likely to follow in a similar manner. Moreover, when one's comrades come to visit, it will be unsightly if all the members of one's household are in disarray.

When one is performing his duties, he should not just simply appear before the master. He should wait for a moment in the next room, check his colleagues' appearances, and then go in to audience. If it is not done this way, his effort will likely be in vain.

When one has been addressed by the master, even though he is seated at a distance he should quickly answer, "Yes!" draw forward immediately approaching on his knees, and make his response with full respect. He should thereupon quickly withdraw, prepare his answer, and relate the facts as they are. One should not make a display of one's own wisdom. Moreover, according to the circumstances, when one is considering how best to give an answer, he should consult with a man who is adroit at speech. It is a matter of not pushing through one's own personal opinion.

One should not be close by when someone is relating something to the master. It is best to withdraw to the side. Still more, if one gossips or laughs foolishly in such a place, it goes without saying that he will be avoided by men of high status, and even men of sensitivity within his own rank are likely to turn their backs on him.

There is a saying that goes, "Even though one associates with many people, he should never cause discord." In all things one should support others.

When one has the least bit of spare time, he should always take out some piece of literature or something with characters on it that he has kept in his pocket, and read where no one will be looking. Characters are such that if one is not used to them both waking and sleeping, they will soon be forgotten.
The writing of characters is also like this.

When one is going by the place where the elders are in attendance to the master, he should stoop a bit and place his hands to the ground as he passes. To be without deference and simply stamp through the area would be outrageously rude. To be a samurai is to be polite at all times.

One should not tell a lie, no matter to whom he is speaking or how little is said. Even the most trivial matters should be shown as they are. If one tells a lie, it will become a habit, and in the end he will be forsaken by others. One should understand that to be questioned by others can bring on shame for a lifetime.

A person who has not studied poetry is the poorer for this lack, and thus one should study it. One should always be genteel in his speaking. A man shows his inmost self by a single word.

In the intervals of one's work, one should learn horsemanship. After becoming well-founded in the basics, other techniques should follow with training.

If one would seek good companions, he will find them among those with whom he studies Learning and calligraphy. Harmful companions to avoid will be found among those who play go, chess, and *shakuhachi.*[2] There is no shame in not knowing these latter amusements. Indeed, they are matters to be taken up only in the stead of wasting one's time completely.

A person's good and evil are dependent on his companions. When three people are together there will always be an exemplary person among them, and one should choose the good person and follow his example. Looking at the bad person, one should correct his own mistakes.

When one has some spare time and returns to his home, he should walk around the stables and rear areas mending the walls and fences and filling the places where the dogs have been digging. Ignorant maids and the like will pull the leaves under the eaves and burn them, doing only what is needed for the present, but will not know what to do after that. One should have a deep understanding that all things are like this.

At six o'clock in the evening one should close his gate tightly and not open it again except to let people in and out. Not to do so is negligence, and will inevitably invite disaster.

At night, one should go about himself checking the fires in the kitchen and living room, and make firm instructions concerning them. Other than that, he should make instructions nightly in order to form habits in caution against spreading fires. Women of both high and low ranks have no feelings for such things, and will leave household goods and clothing spread around, and be greatly negligent. One should not think he can hire others and have them do everything, but rather he should be of the mind to rely on himself and to know the condition of things. Only then should he delegate to others.

It is hardly necessary to record that both Learning and the military arts are the Way of the Warrior, for it is an ancient law that one should have Learning on the left and the martial arts on the right. But this is something that will not be obtainable if one has not prepared for it beforehand.

Notes

[1] From the Confucian *Book of Odes.*

[2] A five-holed bamboo flute played vertically.

THE RECORDED WORDS OF ASAKURA SOTEKI

"A general of great merit should be said to be a man who has met with at least one great defeat."

THE RECORDED WORDS OF ASAKURA SOTEKI

Asakura Norikage
(1474-1555 A.D.)

Asakura Norikage was the mainstay of the Asakura clan during the difficult years of the Ikko sect uprisings in Echizen and continued instability in the nearby area of the capital. Though never a daimyo himself, he was advisor to three generations of Asakura chieftains and spent most of his life in military campaigns. In 1548 he shaved his head and became a priest, taking the name of Soteki. Neither the years nor religion deterred him from his occupation, however, for at the age of 79 he marched with his army to the province of Kaga for what was to be his last campaign against the Ikko adherents. On September 8 of that year, he died in camp of natural causes.

The Soteki Waki *is a collection of his sayings, written down by a close retainer a few years before his death. It consists of 83 precepts or anecdotes and is written in a* kanamajiri *style. In this record we can see the legacy of Asakura's practicality and vision. The idealism of former and later ages is lacking here, for "though a*

*warrior be called a dog or a beast, what is basic for him is to win."
In this connection, Asakura stressed the mutual fates of master
and retainer, and thus the need for harmonious relations between
them. Almost all of the precepts here point to success on the battlefield in one way or another, whether outwardly concerned with
morality or feeding one's horse, and clearly reflect an active general's concerns and experiences.*

The Recorded Words of Asakura Soteki

It is a failure on the part of a general to forcibly send his troops
to attack a castle, whether on mountain or flatland. This would be
sending his valuable troops to die before his very eyes. This matter
comes first in a general's considerations.

In connection with military matters, one must never say that
something can absolutely not be done. By this, the limitations of
one's heart will be exposed.

In attacking enemy-held ground, one should never assume that
his opponents will not hold their own. If, in such an attack, the
enemy stiffly resisted, one's entire forces would be disheartened.

From time to time a man should soak hard soy beans in water
and feed them to his horse. There will be no pots or pans for such
things on the battlefield.

No matter how lacking a man may be in humanity, if he would
be a warrior, he should first of all tell no lies. It is also basic that
he be not the least bit suspicious, that he habitually stand on in-
tegrity, and that he know a sense of shame. The reason being that
when a man who has formerly told lies and acted suspiciously par-
ticipates in some great event, he will be pointed at behind his back
and neither his allies nor his enemies will believe in him, regardless
of how reasonable his words may be. One should be very prudent
about this.

During any military affair, no matter how important the event may be, when something is communicated by word of mouth, the least bit of vagueness will invite grievous results.

A few years past, at the battle of Minatogawa in Kaga, there were more than 500 heads taken. From these, the heads of very young men were separated, receivers from the enemy beckoned, and the heads returned quickly. In the fight between foot soldiers previous to that, however, no such thing was done.[1]

At the time of a great battle or distressing retreat, the enemy may send out troops to exacerbate a general in various ways in order to judge his present feelings. He should not show the least bit of weakness, however, or let out a single word. One should be careful about this and not be negligent.

Though a warrior may be called a dog or beast, what is basic for him is to win.

A man who keeps a considerable number of retainers—and this goes without saying for a general—should first of all have the religious and habitual awareness to provide for his men well. Especially for men who have been long in service, but also for those who are new or presently employed, if there is a retainer who has died in the midst of dutiful service and leaves behind a young child, the master should treat that child with great care, dealing with it kindly in a way that it will be able to become an adult. When a samurai by chance has no natural heir, if the master will encourage him to take on a fitting adopted child while he and his wife are yet healthy, and advise him in a way that his family line will not run out, even a childless man will feel reassured and grateful, and will not hold back his life for his master. If a man will kindly do such things, those under him will feel greatly blessed, and those who hear and see these things will think of him as reliable. Those under his command will naturally serve him with great loyalty, as will those of other clans, and he will have many reliable retainers.

A master will incur the punishment inflicted on his retainers, and his retainers will incur that inflicted on their master. Master and retainer together should not be negligent.

A master should not unreasonably make requests for the possession of his retainers, such as their horses and falcons, or their swords, halberds, paintings or Chinese goods. Generally speaking, for retainers to possess valuable articles is the same as if the master himself possessed them. If in spite of that, however, the master should still desire something, he should offer double its appropriate price. If this is not done, those retainers who hear or see such acts will lose their desire to have such things; and, in the end, famous articles that have been handed down from generations past will be sent off to other provinces. One should be very discriminating about this.

When one has summoned his retainers or is treating them to some small dishes, it will not do to pick out one or two men for special treatment.

It is not good to be feared by one's own retainers. It has been passed down from ages past that it is fundamental to value one's retainers' deep devotion. If such is not the case, when the time comes it will be difficult for them to be valuable to you by throwing away their lives.

One should understand well that if a master begins to feel that he is despised by his retainers, he will very soon go mad. How could one who is supposedly of a position not even to be despised by the enemy, be looked down upon by his own men? Such a thing is truly laughable. It is, moreover, the basis of bringing confusion to the clan.

There were to Lord Eirin's[2] character many high points difficult to measure, but according to the elders the foremost of these was the way he governed the province by his civility. It goes without saying that he acted this way toward those in the samurai class, but he was also polite in writing letters to the farmers and townspeople, and even in addressing these letters he was gracious beyond normal practice. In this way, all were willing to sacrifice their lives for him and become his allies.

Lady Keishitsu[3] used to relate that Lord Eirin constantly commanded, "Little Norikage has been raised as a spoiled child, and therefore is likely to act impolitely to the samurai after we are gone. From time to time teach him manners."

As a human being, a man must save for the future. It has been handed down from the beginning, however, that as a samurai, one should not be like the wealthy, hoarding excesses of money, gold and silver, and making savings one's foundation. Still, Hojo Soun of Izu⁴ hoarded away in his warehouse articles as small as a pin. Munenaga used to relate, however, that Soun was the kind of man who would even break up precious jewels for use in times of war.

A man who would have a gardener do a carpenter's job, or a carpenter do a gardener's job, is no judge of men and is highly incompetent. No matter how bright a person is, he will have his strong and weak points. If one will comply with men's various abilities and use them appropriately, all matters will be assigned correctly and the master will be without trouble.

For a warrior, there is nothing distressing about hearing of something and fleeing. To see something and flee, however, is a great evil.

In having the fortune of the gods in martial affairs, it is fundamental for a samurai, regardless of his character, to gain fame in skill while he is yet young. For those who gained a reputation for being unskilled while young and yet gained skill as adults are few and far between. Moreover, even if a man who has been known as skillful in his youth shows a lack of skill as an adult, it will do no damage to his reputation for awhile. Thus, it is essential to have prudence in such matters.

A general of great merit should be said to be a man who has met with at least one great defeat. A man like myself who has gone his whole life with victories alone and suffered no defeats cannot be called a man of merit, even though he gains in years.

Concerning seasickness, we once all said that if we fixed our minds on the fact that the enemy was waiting on the shore, there would not be a one of us to get sick. A few years ago when we took a great force by ship to Tamba, as we had anticipated, not a single man got sick. On the return trip, however, everyone got seasick.

It is a truly sympathetic matter when a man who was born thick-witted works seriously with all his heart. However, when a man who has simply a common understanding of things and yet considers himself to be far more clever than others does something vulgar, inexcusable or unjust, he is being truly rude, hateful, and deserving of heavy punishment. This has nothing to do with social position.

For a warrior, there is nothing distressing about hearing of something and fleeing. To see something and flee, however, is a great evil. Doing such, one will be doing nothing other than having his forces wiped out to a man. To hear of certain conditions and retreat is one sort of stratagem, and thus is not really a matter of fleeing. It has been said in both former times and present that, generally speaking, in a great retreat if one does not withdraw in unity and while striking the enemy, his retreat will fail. For such a reason it has been said that it is fundamental to "let one's ear be a coward, and his eyes a hero."

Notes

[1] This anecdote emphasizes that sympathy is one of the traits of a true man. The families of the vanquished young warriors would have been very grateful for this service.

[2] Asakura Ujikage, Soteki's father or older brother. There is some question of delineation; some have Ujikage, others Toshikage, as Soteki's father.

[3] Soteki's mother.

[4] See previous chapter.

THE IWAMIZUDERA MONOGATARI

"Learning is to a man as the leaves and branches are to a tree, and it can be said that he should simply not be without it."

THE IWAMIZUDERA MONOGATARI

Takeda Shingen
(1521-1573 A.D.)

Takeda Harunobu, or Takeda Shingen, was one of the best-known generals of the Warring States Period, famous as a strategist and for his many battles with Uesugi Kenshin at Kawanaka-jima. His father, Takeda Nobutora, had unified the province of Kai, but in a succession issue in 1541 he was driven from its territory by his son, who now assumed authority as daimyo.

From this time until his death, Takeda Shingen was involved in the continuing national struggle for supremacy. He was constantly harassed in the north by Uesugi Kenshin and in the west by the combined forces of Oda Nobunaga and Tokugawa Ieyasu. In 1551 he shaved his head, took the name of Shingen, and entered religion. His rival Uesugi did the same in 1552. In 1571, Shingen answered the summons of the Ashikaga shogun, Yoshiakira, and formed an alliance with the Asai and Asakura clans and the monks of the Honganji in order to move against the forces of Oda. In 1573, still in the midst of this campaign, he was struck by a bullet[1] and died a few days later.

Takeda Shingen received fame as a tactician, fief administrator and diplomat. He relied on his judgment of individuals' abilities and the formation of alliances rather than on castles and fortifications. A poem attributed to him runs:

> Men are your castles
> Men are your walls
> Sympathy is your ally
> Enmity your foe.

Yet he was a strict disciplinarian as a warrior, and there is an exemplary story in the Hagakure *relating his execution of two brawlers, not because they had fought, but because they had not fought to the death. It is not surprising to learn that he was an avid reader of* Sun Tzu *and* Han Fei Tzu.

The selection given here is from the 40th chapter of the Koyogunkan, *a book written long after Takeda's death by Kosaka Masanobu, his close retainer. In it are related the history and battles of the Takeda clan along with anecdotes and explanations of old customs. The 40th chapter, often called the* Iwamizudera Monogatari, *preserves many of Takeda's discussions on human nature that took place with his retainers at the Iwamizu Temple in his home province of Kai. His stories are often long and sometimes troublesome, but manifest clearly his emphasis on the value of discrimination and foresight, and perhaps indicate the expansive personality he was said to have had.*

The Iwamizudera Monogatari

One night Lord Shingen again spoke to those around him, saying, "regardless of whether a man's rank be high or low, there is one thing that will make it replete. Can any of you guess what that is?" After a while they all spoke up saying that they could not discern what it might be, no matter how much they thought about it. Shingen then said, "If only a man will not do what he himself would like to do, and do those things that he finds unpleasant, his position, no matter what it is, will be replete."

One night Lord Shingen said, "It is the act of a man of low rank to prune off an astringent persimmon and graft a sweet one to it. A samurai of middle or upper rank, and particularly the lord of a province, would find many uses for an astringent persimmon precisely because of its nature. This does not mean, however, that one should cut down a sprig that has already been grafted. Are not all things like this?''

A man with deep far-sightedness will survey both the beginning and the end of a situation and continually consider its every facet as important.

Lord Shingen said, ''In this world, not only samurai, but also servants down through the lower classes are born with differing characters, and people are apt to misjudge them by appearance. First, men with discrimination[2] will be viewed as schemers; second, men with deep far-sightedness[3] will be seen as cowards; and third, men with rough behavior will be mistaken for real warriors. These are great errors.

''A man with discrimination will leave off 70 percent of a matter, and speak of only the remainder.

''A man with deep far-sightedness will survey both the beginning and end of a situation and continually consider its every facet as important. When speaking up about something according to the results as he projects them, he will think of his wife and children beforehand and thus judge the situation in real terms. This is called far-sightedness. Men who do not have this quality view those who do as cowards, and are surely less mature.

''Again, a man who behaves with rough manner has neither discrimination nor far-sightedness, speaks unreasonably, and considers the terseness of the far-sighted and discriminating man as pusillanimity. When the time of battle has arrived, however, he thinks of his wife and children for the first time; and when his moment has come, his end will no doubt be wanting. Thus is rough behavior on the very verge of cowardice.''

Lord Shingen said, ''Because this man with rough behavior has neither discrimination nor far-sightedness, he further has not much of a sense of shame. Thus, even if his father and brothers were suddenly killed and the enemy apparent, contrary with his usual roughness, he would have no thought of striking that enemy at all. When competing in battle, the man with rough behavior will inevitably fall short of even the run of the mill, and yet will make up various excuses and justifications for himself. This is entirely because he lacks both discrimination and far-sightedness."

Again one night Lord Shingen said, "Just as contrivance and meditation are different, so are discrimination and quick-wittedness. This can be understood by the fact that in this world there are those who have a sense of discrimination but are not quick-witted, and there are also those who are quick-witted but have no sense of discrimination. If this is not explained clearly, young people will remain none the wiser; so for their sake let us put it into other words. Discrimination is performed by the mind, while quick-wittedness is a function of *ch'i (ki)*. Oversights are rare with people who have discrimination, but those who lack this quality and are only quick-witted will make many mistakes. This critique should be common among men of knowledge, but unlearned youth will rarely understand it."

Once Lord Shingen said, "It is essential for a man to have far-sightedness; for, having this quality, he will also have a sense of discrimination. When a man thinks through to the conclusion of things and is still unable to make his own discernment, if he is of high rank he may consult one of the capable elders, if of lower rank he may discuss the matter with the capable acquaintances he has among his relatives and comrades. Coming to a conclusion in this way, mistakes will be few. Thus, it is my humble opinion that far-sightedness is the foundation of discrimination.

"Generally, if men have a deep far-sightedness, are quick-witted, and are able to discern situations well, no matter to what problems they may apply themselves, their fame will remain to later generations. There is, for example, the legend of how Fujiwara Fuhito regained a great crystal gem from the bottom of the sea with his discrimination and quick-wittedness. Using these qualities, Fuhito pledged his love to a sea nymph, begging her to dive into the sea and bring the gem to him. Although such means might be called duplicity, his discernment and far-sightedness are obviously praiseworthy, for with this gem the fire of the sun and moon were obtained, and water procured. At the foundation in this case, too, was a quick awareness, both contriving and thoughtful.

"Be this as it may, there is but one thing concerning which all one's discrimination and quick-wittedness will never bring about successful contrivance or meditation. Each one of you try to tell what that is!"

None of those listening could think of anything, so Shingen laughed and said, "Man's life shrinks away, and there is little to be done about it."

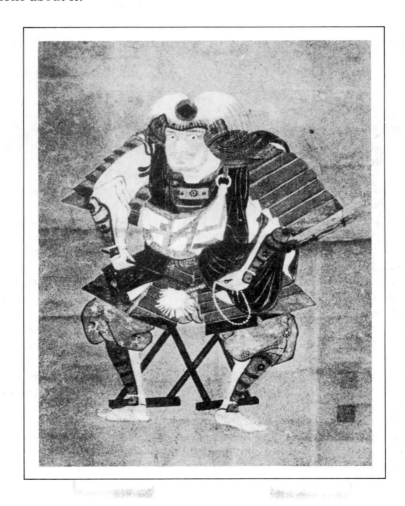

One night, Lord Shingen quoted from an old proverb, and said, "Chen K'ung said to Emperor Wen of the Wei, 'Encountering another, it is best to speak only a third part of what you have to say, and not yet open your heart completely. When a man is self-composed, he does not become completely intimate with another; when a flower is composed, it does not bloom all at once although the spring has come. Otherwise, yesterday's friend will become today's enemy, as yesterday's flower will become today's dust.' Thus, when one is speaking with a man about some deep matter and leaves off seven parts to speak only three, it is entirely to keep shame at a distance. But when one explains to a man lacking in discrimination that it is bad to speak out abruptly, he ends up not speaking at all. Likewise, a man who finds import in all things considers it bad to graft sweet persimmons to a tree that bears astringent fruit. Explain this to a man of little understanding, however, and he will cut off the graft that has long borne sweet fruit, once again grafting on a puckery one . . . all with an air of clear understanding. This is bringing on bad results with the intention of doing good, and is the manner of men who are lacking in discrimination. An old proverb says, 'A little piece of gold may be highly valued, but if it gets in one's eye, the result will be darkness.' Isn't this about the same?"

One night Lord Shingen said, "Learning[4] is to a man as the leaves and branches are to a tree, and it can be said that he should simply not be without it. Learning is not only reading books, however, but is rather something that we study to integrate with our own way of life. One who was born in the house of a warrior, regardless of his rank or class, first acquaints himself with a man of military feats and achievements in loyalty, and, listening to just one of his dictums each day, will in a month know 30 precepts. Needless to say, if in a year he learns 300 precepts, at the end of that time he will be much for the better. Thus, a man can divide his mind into three parts: he should throw out those thoughts that are evil, take up those ideas that are good, and become intimate with his own wisdom. Doing this, he should have little to shame him.

"I would honor and call wise the man who penetrates this principle, though he lacks the knowledge of a single Chinese character. As for those who are learned in other matters, however, I would avoid them regardless of how deep their knowledge might be. That is how shallow and untalented this monk[5] is.''

Once, Lord Shingen said, "In this world there are many kinds of men. There are those who have discrimination but no quick wit; those who are quick-witted but lack compassion; and those who have compassion, but not the ability to judge one man from the next. There are many—eight out of ten—in the reverenced upper classes who are useless in distinguishing one man from the next. Among those intimate with each other in the lower ranks, there are almost none at all.

"Thus, there are many different kinds of men, and if we look at this fact from a different angle we can see that their differences stem from having minds lacking in discrimination. If only a man will excel in discrimination, he will do well in any other field— quick-wittedness, far-sightedness, the ability to distinguish one man from another, and gaining in merit. Thus a man should know that discrimination is the foundation of all these other qualities. To improve his own sense of this quality, he should make it his aim each morning and his meditation each night.''

Lord Shingen said, "When one is employing samurai from the time they are children, and looks ahead to their qualities as adults, there will generally be four differing types. Suppose that three samurai—one who has much experience in the Way of the Warrior, one who is very valiant, and one who is exceptionally clever at things—get together and talk over stories of warriors, military exploits, etc., in the company of four children.

"The first child will just sit with his mouth open and look at the speaker's face. The second will strain his ears and listen with his face inclined a little to the floor. The third will look at the speaker's face and listen, laughing periodically with a cheerful look about him. The fourth will get up and leave. These are the various types.

"First, the child who sits listening as though in a dream will, as time goes on, slacken in dispostion, and, no matter how many times he is involved in military affairs, will remain incapable of discerning the situation. As his behavior will be without focus or continuity, he will not retain fitting and proper advisors, but will rather listen to the opinions of his good friends.

"Second, the child who listened to the stories of warriors with strained ears will be no problem in the future. He will become like those men with knowledge of martial affairs who served Yokota, a governor of Bitchu; Hara, governor of Mino; Obata, the Nyudo of Yamashiro, and Tada, the governor of Awaji during Nobutada's[6] generation; and Yamamoto Kansuke and Hojo Ujiyasu in my own time.

"Third, the child who listened to the stories while laughing in an amused manner, in the future will inevitably become praised for his martial exploits. He will, however, go too far and become haughty, thus receiving people's spite.

"Fourth, the child who got up and left during the stories of warriors, will in the future, eight or nine times out of ten, become a coward. Even the two or three who do not become cowards will follow behind others. Such a man will walk about speaking with great authority and think of himself as worthy of great martial fame if he simply strikes off the head of a fleeing enemy who has fallen behind his own ranks in battle. If a real warrior has performed a true deed of merit, this man will imagine that although this feat, like his own, was in striking down a worthy enemy, the warrior's reputation as a brave man rests on the intercession of others. Thinking that men in this world are not so different from one another, he will resent the real warrior, and let his mouth wag freely. Thus will one who left the discussions of warriors as a child, turn out on becoming an adult."

Once Lord Shingen said, "When the daimyo who rule an entire province employ men, they fancy only a certain kind of samurai, and respect those with the same behavior and deportment. These they employ and treat well, but I myself deplore such an attitude.

"My reason is that when a samurai of rank, either high or low, first learns the natural way of playing *kemari*,[7] he sets up the four boundary marks in his garden.

"Particularly in spring, the cherry blossoms break out in color and the willow darkens with green. When the spring passes and these two trees have finished with their competition, summer comes, and at length goes by. With autumn, the leaves of the maple turn red, sad that they soon will fall. Though they are sung in various ways through the mist of the evenings and the autumnal rains, when winter is at hand not a one of them remains.

Just at that time the eternally unchanging color of the pine manifests itself. It is like this, too, in the world of men; and thus the provincial lord who fancies only one kind of man is absolutely to be censured.

"However, it is laudable, I suppose, when a good general recruits only one kind of retainer. Three times four equals 12, after all, but three plus four only seven."

Notes

[1] Guns were first introduced to the Japanese in 1542 when a group of Portuguese landed on the southern island of Tanegashima. Firearms were called "tanegashima" for a long time thereafter.

[2] *Funbetsu:* possibly translated as "judgment" or "wisdom," it consists of two characters meaning to divide or separate; thus, to see one thing clearly from another. Takeda felt that this was the greatest quality a man could have.

[3] *Enryo:* literally, to think far into the future; hence, to act with hesitancy or reserve.

[4] This refers not so much to scholastic endeavors as to a basic education in Confucianism, perhaps much like the medieval classical education in Latin and Greek.

[5] In 1551, Takeda shaved his head and became a lay monk of the Zen sect, taking the name Shingen.

[6] Shingen's father.

[7] A game like football. Traditionally, the boundaries of the playing field were marked by a cherry tree in the northeast corner, a willow in the southeast corner, a maple in the southwest corner, and a pine in the northwest corner.

OPINIONS IN
NINETY-NINE ARTICLES

"One's soldiers should not yell abuse at the enemy. An old saying goes, 'Arouse a bee and it will come at you with the force of a dragon.'"

OPINIONS IN NINETY-NINE ARTICLES

Takeda Nobushige
(1525-1561 A.D.)

Takeda Nobushige was the second son of Takeda Nobutora, and it was to him that his father had wanted to pass on the fief when Takeda Shingen revolted. Nobushige is said to have sided with Shingen in this matter, and Shingen, for his part, supported Nobushige after this event and placed great faith in him, entrusting him with much of the fighting in Shinano. At the battle of Kawanakajima in 1561, Shingen's main force had been out-maneuvered by Uesugi Kenshin, and Shingen himself was in danger when Nobushige with his small force arrested the enemy advance of about 3,000 men. Shingen's headquarters were saved, but Nobushige was cut down in the action and died at the age of 37.

The Ninety-Nine Articles were written down by Takeda Nobushige three years before his death for the benefit of his son. Written in kanbun, *they are a tour de force of the educated warrior, each precept followed by a relevant quote, usually from a Chinese classic. There is no particular order, and the subject matter ranges from injunctions against carrying a dull sword to encouraging belief in the gods and Buddhas.*

This selection from Takeda's work was also included in the Koyogunkan *as a part of the Takeda clan's legacy. The* Koyogunkan *is given two chapters in this study because it was probably the most widely read book of bushi origin during the Edo Period, and because it was appended and put into its present form[1] by Obata Kagenori (1572-1663), from whose school of martial studies a number of important writers and philosophers emerged, among them Daidoji Yuzan and Yamaga Soko. Obata himself was the son of one of Shingen's retainers, employed by the Tokugawa after the Takeda clan's demise. After disciplining himself in the martial arts, he took leave of the Tokugawa and traveled the country, testing himself. He participated at both the battle of Sekigahara and the fall of Osaka Castle, thus receiving much of his knowledge of martial affairs first hand.*

Opinions in Ninety-Nine Articles from Kotenkyu to His Son and the Elders (Selections)

One must never be perfidious to his master. In the *Lun Yu* it says, "One should act according to the Way even in times of haste. One should act according to the Way even in times of danger." It says further, "When one is serving his master, he should exert himself."

One should not exhibit the least bit of cowardice on the battlefield. In the *Wu Tzu* it says, "He who would save his life shall lose it, and he who would give up his life shall save it."

One should take care in his activities so that he will be without negligence. In the *Shih Chi* it says, "If the master acts correctly, his retainers will perform well, even if given no commands. But if the master acts incorrectly, even though he gives commands they will not be followed."

One should exert himself in the martial arts absolutely. In the *San Lueh* it says, "There are no weak soldiers under a strong general."

One should not tell a lie in any situation whatsoever. In the oracles of the gods it has been said, "Although truth may not be rewarded at once, in the end it will receive the compassion of the gods and Buddhas." In battle, however, shouldn't one act according to the circumstances of the moment? In the *Sun Tzu* it says, "Avoid the enemy's strength, strike at his weakness."[2]

One should not be the least bit unfilial toward his parents. In the *Lun Yu* it says, "In serving one's parents, one should use all his strength."

One should never treat his brothers carelessly. In the *Hou Han Shu* it says, "One's brothers are his right and left hands."

One should not utter a word about his own inadequacies. In the *Oko* it says, "When a man lets out a single word, the long and short of him will be known."

One should not use rough manners with anyone. With priests, women, children, the poor, and the elderly, one should be all the more polite. It is said in the *Li Chi* that, "One is safe when polite, but in danger when ill-mannered."

It is essential to develop one's self in the martial arts. In the *Lun Yu* it says, "To study the heretical will only be damaging."

One must not be negligent in Learning. In the *Lun Yu* it says, "To study and not to think is darkness. To think without study is dangerous."

One should endeavor not to be negligent in any matter concerning deportment. In the *Lun Yu* it says, "When Confucius entered the ancestral temple of the Chou, he asked about everything."

One should not be excessive in refined pleasures. In *Shih Chi* it says, "When the banquet is in full swing, there will be confussion. When pleasure is at its height, sorrow appears. In the *Tso Chuan* it says, "High living is like drinking poisoned sake: it is unthinkable." Again, it says in the *Lun Yu*, "One should respect virtue as he loves a beautiful woman."

In matters both great and small, one should not turn his back on his master's commands. In the *Lun Yu* it says, "Water will conform to the shape of the vessel that contains it, whether it be round or square."

One should not ask for gifts or enfiefments from the master. In the *Tso Chuan* it says, "Reward without merit is unjust gain, and is an invitation to disaster."

One should neither grumble nor gossip. In the *Lun Yu* it says, "One should not flatter because he is poor, or be haughty because he is rich."

One should not turn his back on reproof.

It is essential to act with compassion toward one's retainers. In the *San Lueh* it says, "Using the people is like using one's own hands and feet."

When a retainer is ill, one should go to visit the man with real concern, even though it may cause one some inconvenience. In the *Chun Ch'an* it says, "One should attend to his warriors as he would to his own thirst."

One should not forget his retainer's loyal deeds. In the *San Lueh* it says, "When good and bad are considered the same, retainers of merit will lose interest."

One should not turn his back on reproof. In the words of the ancients, "Good medicine is bitter to the mouth, but has effect on the disease. Faithful words hurt one's ears, but have value for one's conduct." Moreover, in the *Shu Ching* it says, "When the wood follows the inkline, it will be straight. When the master follows a remonstrance, he will become a sage.''

When one's retainers are not without loyalty, and for some unavoidable circumstances are in difficult straits, the master should give them assistance for a while. An old proverb says, "If one plans to abide in a place for one year, he should plant the five grains. If his plan is for ten years, he should plant trees. If one's plans are for his whole life, there is nothing like sustaining his retainers.''

One should not go in and out of the palace by the back gate on his own business. An old saying has it, "Father and son do not sit in the same rank, nor do men and women sit together.''

A man who has been alienated from his friends should make endeavors in the Way of humanity. In the *Lun Yu* it says, "One should not deviate from the path of humanity for even the time it takes to eat his meal.''

One must not be rude when being questioned about things by another. In the *Lun Yu* it says, "When one is mixing with friends, should not his words be sincere?''

One should not be lazy in attending to his everyday duties. In the *Lun Yu* it says, "If one has energy left after endeavoring in virtue, he should study.''

Note: When one is attending his duties, he should at first go to where his fellows are gathered, and later withdraw to the rear. In short, it is essential for a person to consider well where he should be. There is a saying of the ancients that goes, "One should not think that his companions will be the same after not meeting them for three days. This is true all the more for a Gentleman.''[3]

No matter how intimate one may be with another, he should not gossip about trifling things in front of him. There is a saying of the ancients that goes, "Think over a matter three times before letting out a word; think it over nine times before acting.''

One should make endeavors in Zen meditation. There is a saying of the ancients that goes, "There is no particular secret to Zen. It is simply making a settlement of the matter of life and death.''

One should on no account tell people of other clans about the wrong-doings that have occurred in one's own. There is a saying that goes, "Good news never leaves the gate, but bad news travels a thousand miles."

At no matter what time of the day one returns to his home, he should send a messenger ahead of him announcing his return. When one comes home suddenly and witnesses the negligence of his servants, he will have to rebuke them. Moreover, if one made a searching examination into the details of such matters, would there ever be an end to them? In the *Lun Yu* it says, "It is criminal to pass the death sentence without first instructing about right and wrong."

No matter how unreasonably the master may treat a man, he should not feel disgruntled. In the *Hsiao Ching* it says, "Although one may think that the master is unfitting for his position, a retainer must do the work of a retainer." It is also said that, "The man who hunts a deer does not gaze at the mountains." It is further said that, "An underling does not pass judgments on a superior."

Concerning the chastisements of servants, if the crime is small, it should be left off with a rebuke. For a grave offense there is no doubt that a man should lose his life. Chiang Shih[4] said, "If one would prevent the bud from leafing, he must, in the end, use an ax."
Note: If the death sentence is passed often for simply lesser crimes, will not men lose their wills, according to the circumstances? In the *Lu Shih Ch'un Ch'iu* it says, "If the law is too strict, it will not be listened to; if prohibitions are many, they cannot be carried out."

One should not levy on the farmers more than their predetermined amount of labor duty. In the *Chun Ch'an* it says, "If there is oppression from above, there will be disruption below. If the people are heavily exploited, there will be no end to death sentences and they will kill each other off."

In the presenting of awards, no matter whether it is great or small, it should be done at once. In the *San Lueh* it says, "In the reward of merit, time should not pass by."

In putting people to use, one should assign them tasks according to their abilities. There is a saying of the ancients that goes, "A good carpenter will not throw wood away; a good general will not discard a warrior."

There is a saying of the ancients that goes, "It is painful to hear the gong commanding a retreat, but a joy to hear the one that announces an advance."

One should not be negligent in having his armor in good order. There is a saying of the ancients that goes, "A nine-story tower begins with the foundation."

When heading for the front, one should not be even a day behind the commander. There is a saying of the ancients that goes, "It is painful to hear the gong commanding a retreat, but a joy to hear the one that announces an advance."

One should groom his horse well. In the *Lun Yu* it says, "As a dog protects a man, and a horse labors in his stead, they are animals that do him good service."

When facing opposing forces, one should attack the place that has not yet been secured. There is a saying of the ancients that goes, "The man who defeats the enemy often is he who does not win by means of formation." There is another saying that goes, "It is the custom of our clan to simply dash in at full speed, and give the enemy no respite."

During a battle, one should not chase the enemy far. In the *Szu Ma Fa* it says, "In chasing the enemy, one should not leave the ranks. By doing so he will bring confusion to his unit, lose order in his column, and waste men and horses."

If one's forces are winning a battle, it is better to push right on through without giving the enemy a chance to rally. While all of the enemy forces have still not been crushed, there is yet a chance for them to recover. In the *San Lueh* it says, "An attack is like the rising of the wind."

One should not praise the vastness or strength of the enemy in front of others. In the *San Lueh* it says, "One should not allow a man to speak of the good points of the enemy."

One's soldiers should not yell abuse at the enemy. An old saying goes, "Arouse a bee and it will come at you with the force of a dragon."

When a battle is approaching, one should treat his men roughly. Their anger thus accumulated, they will fight fiercely. In the *Szu Ma Fa* it says, "When one is dealing with a weak and powerless person, he should handle that person as though handling water. When dealing with the powerful and mighty, he should use the same respect as when handling fire."

One should never display a weak attitude, even though he may be with sympathetic relatives or retainers. In the *San Lueh* it says, "If a man loses his courage, his servants and soldiers will lose their respect for him."

One should not be fond of maneuvering too much. There is a saying of the ancients that goes, "Wishing for too much, one will, in the end, get nothing. Why be fond of going too far from what is natural?" Moreover, in the *Lun Yu* it says, "Excess is the same as insufficiency."

When one would make a surprise attack on the enemy, he should avoid the major roads and seek out the lesser ones. Then attack. An old proverb says, "When easily seen, one should take the by-paths; when not easily seen, the whole army may be moved."

In all things, even though a person asks after one, is it not better to turn a blind eye? In the *Pi Yen Lu* it says, "Even if it is something one likes, it is better to be without it."

One should not fight over every incident that comes along. In the *Lun Yu* it says, "The Gentleman does not contend. If he does, is it not in something like an archery match?"

One should judge good and evil well. In the *San Lueh* it says, "If one good deed is disregarded, the good acts of all will decline. If one evil deed is praised, all will return to evil."

When food provisions arrive at the camp, one should distribute them bit by bit to those in service around him. In the *San Lueh* it says, "When the good generals of long ago were in charge of their soldiers, if wine was sent, they had it all thrown in the river. They then drank water from the streams like everyone else."

If one never makes an effort, it will be difficult to come up in the world. In the *Lao Tzu* it says, "The journey of a thousand miles begins with a single step."

No matter how reasonable one's argument may be, he should not persist in it to a man of high social status. There is a saying that goes, "When words are many, one's position is damaged."

One should not torture himself over a single mistake. What is essential is one's presence of mind hereafter. In the *Lun Yu* it says, "When one makes a mistake, he should not be hesitant to correct it." It says further, "Making a mistake and not correcting it, this is a real mistake."

One should not have contempt for the elderly, regardless of their rank. In the *Lun Yu* it says, "One should respect the elderly as though they were his own parents."

One should not associate with people whose conduct is poor. In the *Shih Chi* it says, "If you don't know a man's character, investigate who his friends are." There is another saying that goes, "A man should not mix only with the high or the low. The bush warbler that flits from flower to flower smells their fragrance without becoming familiar with them."

One should not doubt people too much. In the *San Lueh* it

says, "Vacillation is nothing less than disaster for an army."

One should not criticize the mistakes of others. There is an old saying that goes, "Bestow on others what you yourself are fond of."

One should not carry maliciousness in his heart. In the *Chun Ch'an* it says, "If a malicious man is in a high position, his troops will fight among themselves to the last man."

When summoned by the master, one should not be the least bit tardy. In the *Lun Yu* it says, "When Confucius was summoned by the prince, he went off without waiting for his carriage."

One should not tell secrets to others, whether they be of military plans or otherwise. In the *I Ching* it says, "If the secret is not kept, there will be harm." In the *Shih Chi* it says, "Matters are brought to maturity by means of secrecy, words, when leaked out, are brought to nothing."

One should believe in the gods and Buddhas. There is a saying that goes, "When one is in accord with the Buddha-mind, he will often have strength added to him. The man who defeats others by evil means will in the end fall as he deserves."

When the army of one's allies is at the point of defeat, one should strive all the more. In the *Ku Liang Chuan* it says, "He who lays his strategies well does not fight. He who fights well will not die."

One should use a sharp sword, and should never wear one that is the least bit blunt. It is said that, "A blunt sword will not cut through bones."

One should talk of neither foodstuffs nor trade in front of others. There is an old saying that goes, "Metal is tested by fire; man is tested by what he says."

Even if one should be very intimate with another, he should think carefully before making a request of him. There is a saying of the ancients that goes, "Greedy for one more cup of wine, he loses a whole boatload of fish."

One should not criticize people unnecessarily in the presence of others. In the *Chan Kuo Ts'e* it says, "One should praise another's good points, but not talk about his bad ones."

Even if the enemy's forces are vast, one should attack if their defenses have been neglected. Moreover, one should think carefully before attacking a well-defended enemy, even though his force may be small. In the *Sun Tzu* it says, "One should not attack an imposingly defended camp, nor should he try to obstruct the flag of a well-arranged attack. To strike at such a force, one should keep in mind the suddenness of the snake of Mt. Ch'ang. When its head is struck, the tail comes forth; when the tail is struck, the head comes forth; when its middle is struck, both head and tail are at its attacker. There is a method of attacking such an enemy."

One should not act with a sense of ennui in any matter whatsoever. Mencius said, "If one will earnestly persevere, he will be a follower of Shun."[5]

The above articles are not to be carelessly or repeatedly brought to the ears of others. Rather, this should be thought of as my last testimony for you. Five and two multiplied are ten, but added are only seven. This is a secret oral tradition from the House of Shingen.

> *Eiroku Gannen (1558)*
> *A good day in April*
> *To the House Elders*
> *Takeda Samasuke Nobushige*

Notes

[1] The book was originally written by Kosaka Masanobu (1527-1578), the son of a farmer who rose to be one of Takeda Shingen's most trusted generals.

[2] In the original text there is a play on words here with "truth" and "strength," and with "lie" and "weakness."

[3] The Confucian Gentleman who daily endeavors to study the Way.

[4] The tutor of King Wen of the Chou Dynasty.

[5] One of the three sage kings of ancient China.

LORD NABESHIMA'S
WALL INSCRIPTIONS

"No matter whether a person belongs to the upper or lower ranks, if he has not put his life on the line at least once he has cause for shame."

LORD NABESHIMA'S WALL INSCRIPTIONS

Nabeshima Naoshige
(1538-1618 A.D.)

In 1584, while attempting to extend his domains, the Lord of Hizen was killed in the fighting at Shimabara by the forces of the powerful Shimazu clan. His fief would have soon fallen into the hands of his enemies had it not been for the machinations of his chief retainer, Nabeshima Naoshige, who managed to delude the Shimazu into thinking that resistance to their invasion would be formidable. From that point on, Nabeshima was the real power in the fief.

In 1587 he fought again against the Shimazu and by 1590 was daimyo of Hizen in all but title. During the next ten years he was active in the Korean campaigns, developing a friendship there with Kato Kiyomasa and with Tokugawa Ieyasu upon his return to

Hizen. At the battle of Sekigahara, Nabeshima's son, Katsushige, was persuaded to pit his forces against Tokugawa's, but was quickly recalled by his father and sent instead to attack Tokugawa's enemies in Kyushu, thus saving the clan from disaster.

Nabeshima Naoshige took official command of Hizen in a public and dignified way when the bakufu recognized that the true heir, Ryuzoji Masaie, was not suited for the tasks of a feudal lord. Nabeshima was never officially installed as Lord of Hizen, but allowed that honor to fall to his son, thus avoiding the public censure and reputation of a gekokujo daimyo. Nabeshima faced near-disaster a number of times in his life, yet survived to secure a strong foundation for the perpetuity of his clan. His sayings and activities are recorded in the third chapter of the Hagakure, *a book defining the ideals of the warrior code (written by Yamamoto Tsunetomo, a retainer of Nabeshima's grandson Mitsushige).*

The Wall Inscriptions *were written by a man with a quick intelligence and an ability to grasp the situation, and they are more expressions of everyday wisdom than house laws proper. The author would seem to have been a survivor, rather than a scholar or great tactician. The* Wall Inscriptions *are in diction simple and laconic to the point of being open to interpretation. To remedy this situation, a rather wordy elaboration of* Wall Inscriptions *was written by the 17th-century Confucian scholar Ishida Ittei. The translation used here, however, is based primarily on a direct reading of Nabeshima's work.*

Lord Nabeshima's Wall Inscriptions

Intelligence is the flower of discrimination. There are many examples of the flower blooming but not bearing fruit.

The arts are difficult to master by one's self. When one is unable to produce good judgment, he will for the most part do injury to himself.

Consider the minds of your underlings well, for it will be difficult to be wide of the mark when judging things in comparison from their standpoint.

Encourage and listen well to the words of your subordinates. It is well known that gold lies hidden underground.

The prayers of a descendant should be the memorial services for his ancestors.

The Law is the judgment of subordinates. There is a Principle beyond the faculty of reason.

The consequences of an ancestor's good or evil depends on the receptiveness of his descendants.

Faith is for the cleansing of one's mind, and should not be acted upon so as to disturb the minds of others. Prayer is the hedge that protects this flower.

Coming up in the world should be done in the same way as ascending a stairway.

In all things, think with one's starting point in man.

A man's whole life is determined in his youth. One should act so that his fellows will not lose confidence in him.

A faultfinder will fall into punishment from others.[1]

Great events should be considered lightly.[2]

In all things, think with one's starting point in man.

Do all things with patience.

Written materials miss the essence of reality.

Divination is simply a matter of chance, and relying upon it will likely bring error.[3]

When affairs are carried out lackadaisically, seven out of ten will turn out badly.

During a battle, one should be resolved not to fall into the ploy of the enemy. When one can judge the instant, the victory will definitely be his.

In a fight, one should be rough and reckless. Not so in everyday affairs.[4]

No matter whether a person belongs to the upper or lower ranks, if he has not put his life on the line at least once he has cause for shame.

Everyone should personally know exertion as it is known in the lower classes.

Notes

[1] This might be read as: "Judge not that ye be not judged."

[2] In other words, great events should be thought out thoroughly long before they come to a crisis.

[3] In 1569, Saga Castle was surrounded by a force of 60,000 men under Otomo Sorin. Capitulation was considered, but Nabeshima, at the time a vassal of Ryuzoji Takanobu, suggested a divination. Before the diviner came before Ryuzoji, Nabeshima strictly ordered the man to give a judgment favorable to the defense of the castle. Resistance thus determined, the Otomo forces withdrew.

[4] Another saying of Nabeshima in a similar vein: "Bushido is in being crazy to die. Fifty or more could not kill one such a man." Yamamoto Tsunetomo added, "Great works will not be done with simple determination. One must become insane and crazy to die."

THE LAST STATEMENT OF TORII MOTOTADA

"I will stand off the forces of the entire country here . . . and die a resplendent death."

THE LAST STATEMENT OF TORII MOTOTADA

Torii Mototada
(1539-1600 A.D.)

In the year 1600, Tokugawa Ieyasu was to move east to cam-
paign in Aizu, leaving the strategic Fushimi Castle in the care of
his vassal, Torii Mototada. It was more than likely that the forces
of Ishida Mitsunari, a vassal of the Toyotomi clan in league with
Konishi Yukinaga, would attack this castle after the Tokugawa
forces left. Tokugawa expressed his fear that the castle's forces
were insufficient, but Torii responded that the castle would fall
even if its forces were multiplied ten times, and advocated that his
lord take his troops from the castle's defense and employ them
on his own campaign to the east. The sure destruction of both the
castle and its defenders understood, vassal and lord spent their last
evening together talking over old times.
The inevitable began on August 27 when a large force under
Ishida and Konishi laid siege to the castle. Torii and his defenders
resisted stubbornly, hoping to give Tokugawa more time to make
gains in his march east, and indeed, the fortress was able to hold

*on for over ten days against enormous odds. The end finally came
on September 8 when fire was set to the castle by a traitor from
within. When suicide was recommended by his men, Torii up-
braided them, explaining that now was the time to truly repay
their master's kindness to them, and, with a force of about 300
troops, rushed out of the castle to attack the overwhelming forces
of the enemy. After five such charges, their number was reduced
to ten men and Torii returned to the castle and fell exhausted. A
young samurai from the opposing forces approached and waited
respectfully while the old man committed seppuku and then cut
off his head. The defenders had been cut down to the last man.*

The Last Statement *was written by Torii to his son, Tadamasa,
a few days before the investment of the castle. It is a moving account of unbending and selfless loyalty of vassal to master, and ex-
presses in very clear terms that the true meaning of being a warrior
is to die in battle. In language it is dignified and polite, and yet reveals the strong affection of a father for his son.*

The Last Statement of Torii Mototada

Recently there has been the report of an uprising in the Kamigata area,[1] and that a large number of rebel daimyo who have
fallen into the evil scheming of Ishida Mitsunari will first lay siege
to this castle and are now making such preparations with large
forces. For myself, I am resolved to make a stand within the castle
and to die a quick death. It would not take much trouble to break
through a part of their numbers and escape, no matter how many
tens of thousands of horsemen approached for the attack or by
how many columns we were surrounded. But that is not the true
meaning of being a warrior, and it would be difficult to account as
loyalty. Rather, I will stand off the forces of the entire country
here, and, without even one one-hundredth of the men necessary
to do so, will throw up a defense and die a resplendent death. By
doing so I will show that to abandon a castle that should be defended, or to value one's life so much as to avoid danger and to
show the enemy one's weakness is not within the family traditions
of my master Ieyasu. Thus I will have taken the initiative in causing Lord Ieyasu's other retainers to be resolved, and in advancing

righteousness to the warriors of the entire country. It is not the Way of the Warrior to be shamed and avoid death even under circumstances that are not particularly important. It goes without saying that to sacrifice one's life for the sake of his master is an unchanging principle. As this is a matter that I have thought over beforehand, I think that circumstances such that I am meeting now must be envied by people of understanding.

You, Tadamasa, should understand the following well. Our ancestors have been personal vassals of the Matsudaira[2] for generations. My late father, the Governor of Iga, served Lord Kiyoyasu,[3] and later worked loyally for his son, Hirotada. My older brother, Genshichiro, manifested his absolute loyalty and was cut down in battle at Watari. When the present Lord Ieyasu was a child and sent to Suruga, the Governor of Iga accompanied him as a guardian. Later, at the age of 19, Ieyasu returned to Okazaki, and the Governor of Iga served him with unsurpassed loyalty, living more than 80 years with unswerving steadfastness. Lord Ieyasu, for his part, regarded the Governor as a matchless vassal. When I was 13 and Lord Ieyasu seven, I came before his presence for the first time, and the blessings I have received since must not be forgotten for all the generations to come.

Because Lord Ieyasu is well aware of my loyalty, he has left me here in charge of the important area of Kamigata as Deputy of Fushimi Castle while he advances toward the East, and for a warrior there is nothing that could surpass this good fortune. That I should be able to go ahead of all the other warriors of this country and lay down my life for the sake of my master's benevolence is an honor to my family and has been my most fervent desire for many years.

After I am slain, you must lovingly care for all your younger brothers, beginning with Hisagoro, in my stead. Your younger brothers must earnestly look to you as they would to their father, and must never disobey you. As they grow up, they should one by one present themselves to the Lord Ieyasu, make efforts with their own various talents, do whatever they are commanded, be on friendly terms with one another, and remain forever grateful to their ancestors, by whose blessings our clan was established and its descendants succored. They must be determined to stand with Lord Ieyasu's clan in both its ascent and decline, in times of peace and in times of war; and either waking or sleeping they must never forget that they will serve his clan, and his clan alone. To be avaricious for land or to forget old debts because of some passing dissatisfaction, or to even temporarily entertain treacherous thoughts is not the Way of Man. Even if all the other provinces of Japan were to unite against our lord, our descendants should not set foot inside another fief to the end of time. Simply, in no matter what circumstances, unify with the heart of one family—of elder and younger brothers—exert yourselves in the cause of loyalty, mutually help and be helped by one another, preserve your righteousness and strive in bravery, and be of a mind never to stain the reputa-

tion of a clan that has not remained hidden from the world, but has gained fame in military valor for generations, especially since the days of the Governor of Iga. At any rate, if you will take it into your mind to be sincere in throwing away your life for your master, you will not have the slightest fear or trembling even with the advent of innumerable impending calamities.

I am now 62 years of age. Of the number of times that I have barely escaped death since the time I was in Mikawa I have no idea. Yet, not once have I acted in a cowardly way. Man's life and death, fortune and calamity are in the fate of the times, and thus one should not search out after what he likes. What is essential is to listen to the words of the older retainers, to put to use men of skill and understanding, to not commit acts of adolescent self-will, and to receive the remonstrances of your retainers. The entire country will soon be in the hands of your master, Lord Ieyasu. If this is so, the men who served him will no doubt hope to become daimyo by his appointment. You should know that if such feelings arise, they are inevitably the beginning of the end of one's fortunes in the Way of the Warrior. Being affected by the avarice for office and rank, or wanting to become a daimyo and being eager for such things . . . will not one then begin to value his life? And how can a man commit acts of martial valor if he values his life? A man who has been born into the house of a warrior and yet places no loyalty in his heart and thinks only of the fortune of his position will be flattering on the surface and construct schemes in his heart, will forsake righteousness and not reflect on his shame, and will stain the warrior's name of his household to later generations. This is truly regrettable. It is not necessary to say such a thing, but you should raise the name of your ancestors in this world yet a second time. Moreover, as I have already spoken to you about the management of our clan's affairs, there is no need to speak of that again. You have already seen and heard of what has been regulated from years past.

Be first of all prudent in your conduct and have correct manners, develop harmony between master and retainers, and have compassion on those beneath you. Be correct in the degree of rewards and punishments, and let there be no partiality in your degree of intimacy with your retainers. The foundation of man's duty as a man is in "truth." Beyond this, there is nothing to be said.

Notes

[1] The area of Kyoto and Osaka.

[2] Early in the 13th century, Nitta Yoshisue settled in the village of Tokugawa in Kozuke and took the name of that place for his own. Late in the 14th century, his ninth-generation descendant, Yasuchika, was born in the village of Matsudaira in Mikawa, and took the name of that place for his own line. Ieyasu, Yasuchika's eighth-generation descendant, received permission from the emperor to take the name Tokugawa once again, leaving that of Matsudaira to lateral branches of the family.

[3] Tokugawa's grandfather.

THE PRECEPTS OF
KATO KIYOMASA

"Having been born into the house of a warrior, one's intentions should be to grasp the long and short swords and to die."

THE PRECEPTS OF KATO KIYOMASA

Kato Kiyomasa
(1562-1611 A.D.)

Kato Kiyomasa was born the son of a blacksmith in the province of Owari, and from the age of 18 attached himself to a rising military leader from the same area, Toyotomi Hideyoshi. At age 21, Kato fought at the battle of Shizugadake, earning great honor for his courage, and by his 26th year he was nominated to the lordship of Kumamoto Castle in Kyushu. By 1592 he had earned such respect from Toyotomi that he was awarded partial command of the vanguard invading Korea, along with Konishi Yukinaga and Kuroda Nagamasa. Kato's ferocity quickly became legendary, and it was on this campaign that the Koreans nicknamed him Kishokan, or the "Devil General."

In 1597 Toyotomi again attacked Korea, with Kato once again in command of one segment of the vanguard. Events did not pro-

ceed well for the invaders, but Kato's reputation for courage and obstinacy only increased. Surrounded at a place called Yolsan, he and his troops held out against overwhelming odds—this despite a move by Konishi's forces to sue for peace. Kato never forgot Konishi's betrayal.

Toyotomi's death in 1598 brought the Japanese forces back from Korea, and occasioned a major split among the ruling clans. On one hand were those who ostensibly backed the Toyotomi line, Konishi among them. On the other hand were those who backed the rise of Tokugawa Ieyasu. Despite Kato's long association with Toyotomi, he joined forces with Tokugawa, it is said, for two reasons: Kato recognized that the land would soon fall into Tokugawa's hands, and that Toyotomi's heir would be better off if Kato were on good terms with Tokugawa. Second, Kato wanted to get back at Konishi, who had crossed him in Korea.

After the battle of Sekigahara, during which Kato had stayed in Kyushu ravaging Konishi's lands, Kato met with Tokugawa at the Nijo Castle to discuss the future of Hideyori, the Toyotomi heir. Hideyori was present at the meeting, and it is said that Kato concealed a dirk to use on Tokugawa if the young heir's safety were in question—a bold step when facing the man who was now the de facto ruler of the country. An uneasy truce lasted over the next decade, but in 1611 Kato died at the relatively young age of 50, possibly of poison at the instigation of Tokugawa. The road was now open for the Tokugawa forces, and within a few years the Toyotomi had utterly perished.

Kato's courage and straightforwardness, as well as his ability in castle construction, are legendary. He was a military man first and last, outlawing even the recitation of poetry, putting the martial arts above all else. His precepts show the single-mindedness and Spartan attitudes of the man, and, together with the following selections, demonstrate emphatically that the warrior's first duty in the early 17th century was simply to "grasp the sword and die."

Contemporary accounts of Kato describe him as awe-inspiring, yet not unfriendly, and a natural leader of men. His own words give us a clue to his image. One of his sayings runs: "It is said that the inferior seek to emulate the superior. Thus, if a general slackens only a little, those beneath him will be greatly negligent. Is it not said that the mind of one superior is passed on to 10,000 subordinates?"

The Precepts of Kato Kiyomasa
Articles Concerning which All Samurai
Should be Resolved, Regardless of Rank

One should not be negligent in the way of the retainer. One should rise at four in the morning, practice sword technique, eat one's meal, and train with the bow, the gun, and the horse. For a well-developed retainer, he should become even more so.

If one should want diversions, he should make them such outdoor pastimes as falconing, deer hunting, and wrestling.

For clothing, anything between cotton and natural silk will do. A man who squanders money for clothing and brings his household finances into disorder is fit for punishment. Generally, one should furnish himself with armor that is appropriate to his social position, sustain his retainers, and use his money for martial affairs.

A samurai who practices dancing—which is outside of the martial arts—should be ordered to commit seppuku.

When associating with one's ordinary companions, one should limit the meeting to one host and one guest, and the meal should consist of plain brown rice. When practicing the martial arts, however, one may meet with many people.

As for the decorum at the time of a campaign, one must be mindful that he is a samurai. A person who loves beautification where it is unnecessary is fit for punishment.

The practice of Noh dancing is absolutely forbidden. When one unsheathes his sword, he has cutting a person down in mind. Thus, as all things are born from being placed in one's heart, a samurai who practices dancing—which is outside of the martial arts— should be ordered to commit seppuku.

One should put forth effort in matters of Learning. One should read books concerning military matters, and direct his attention exclusively to the virtues of loyalty and filial piety. Reading Chinese poetry, linked verse, and *waka*[1] is forbidden. One will surely become womanized if he gives his heart knowledge of such elegant, delicate refinements. Having been born into the house of a warrior, one's intentions should be to grasp the long and short swords and to die. If a man does not investigate into the matter of

bushido daily, it will be difficult for him to die a brave and manly death. Thus, it is essential to engrave this business of the warrior into one's mind well.

The above conditions should be adhered to night and day. If there is anyone who finds these conditions difficult to fulfill, he should be dismissed, an investigation should be quickly carried out, it should be signed and sealed that he was unable to mature in the Way of manhood, and he should be driven out.
To this there is no doubt.

To all samurai
Kato Kazuenokami Kiyomasa

Notes

[1] Classical 31-syllable Japanese poetry. Also called *tanka* or "short poetry."

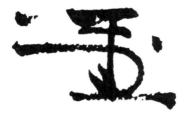

NOTES ON REGULATIONS

"The arts of peace and the arts of war are like the two wheels of a cart which, lacking one, will have difficulty in standing."

NOTES ON REGULATIONS

Kuroda Nagamasa
(1568-1623 A.D.)

Kuroda Nagamasa was the son of a Christian daimyo, Kuroda Josui, and was baptized Simeon in 1583. He was to become well known as a great strategist. While still young, Kuroda was put under the auspices of Oda Nobunaga and later served under Toyotomi Hideyoshi. He participated in the battle of Shizugadake at the age of 15 and later joined the campaign for the pacification of Kyushu. In 1592 and again in 1597 he shared command of the vanguard invasion troops in Korea with Konishi Yukinaga and Kato Kiyomasa. Although he had helped Konishi out of some military tight spots in Korea and was—like Konishi—a Christian, Kuroda supported Tokugawa Ieyasu during the fighting at Sekigahara, and for his efforts was enfieffed at Chikuzen becoming Lord of Fukuoka Castle.

Both Kuroda Nagamasa and his father Josui were well known for their regard for the advice of others, and Nagamasa even set aside one night a month when he would sit with a number of his trusted retainers and allow all to talk freely with the mutual promise that none would become angry over what was said, or gossip about it later. These were called the "Meetings Without Anger."

Although baptized as a Christian at an early age, Kuroda, unlike his father, gave up the faith when it became officially proscribed.

The Regulations *given here were written a year before Kuroda's death to his eldest son, Tadayuki, and the clan elders, and can be found in slightly varying forms in the precepts of his own father, Josui. Kuroda, as do many of the samurai in this book, extols the balance of the arts of peace (Confucian learning and literature) with the arts of war, and encourages fairness and sympathy toward the other three classes of people. His precepts differ from the others in the emphasis he laid on economics, a predisposition he surely inherited from his thrifty father. Most of this material is in concrete terms and has been omitted here. The* Regulations *is a verbose document and the reader can almost feel Kuroda's hesitancy to conclude his advice in the end. His circumspect council was not unheeded by his descendants, however, and the clan continued well into the next chapter of Japanese history.*

Notes on Regulations

If a general who is to maintain the province does not have a special consciousness, his task will be a difficult one to attain. His attitudes must not be the same as the ordinary man's. Firstly, he must be correct in manners and etiquette, must not let self-interest into government, and must take care of the common people. Moreover, he must be prudent in selecting the things that he has interest in; for what the master prefers, all the other warriors will also, and even the farmers and townspeople will take pleasure in them. If he does some trifling thing for pleasure, he should do it in such a manner that it will not cause attention; and he should not forget even for a moment that he is the model for the four classes of people.

Generally speaking, the master of a province should discharge his duties with love and humanity, should not listen to slander, and should exercise the good. His governing should be as clear as the bright sun in the bright sky, and he should think things over deeply in his mind and make no mistakes.

The arts of peace and the arts of war are like the two wheels of a cart which, lacking one, will have difficulty in standing. Naturally, the arts of peace are used during times of tranquility and those of war during times of confusion, but it is most essential to not forget the military during peaceful times nor to disregard scholastics during times of war. When the master of a province feels that the world is in peace and forgets the arts of war, first, military tactics will fall into disuse, the warriors of his clan will naturally become effeminate and lose interest in martial ways, the martial arts will be neglected, the variety of weapons will be insufficient, weapons handed down through generations will become rusty and rot, and there will be nothing of any use during times of emergency. If the Way of the Warrior is thus neglected, ordinary military tactics will not be established; if a military situation were to suddenly arise there would be panic and confusion, consultation would be unprepared for, and the establishment of strategy would be difficult. When one has been born into the house of a military commander, he should not forget the arts of war even for a moment.

Again, what is called cherishing the Way of the Warrior is not a matter of extolling the martial arts above all things and becoming a scaremonger.

Moreover, if scholastics are neglected during the times of war, legislation will be unestablished, self-interest in government will abound, and, as there will be no real love for the members of the clan or the common folk either, the people who carry grudges will be many. Even in the battlefield, if one has only hot-blooded bravery he will not be in accordance with the Way; and being thus unmindful of his soldiers, acts of loyalty will be rare.

Generally speaking, for the master of a domain to cherish the arts of peace is not at all a matter of thinking that he must read many books and write poetry. Rather, it is essential that he know the Way of Truth, that he be particular about his efforts in the scrutinizing of every matter, that he be just in all affairs and make no mistakes, that he be correct in recognizing good and evil and demonstrate rewards and punishments clearly, and that he have a deep sympathy for all people. Again, what is called cherishing the Way of the Warrior is not a matter of extolling the martial arts above all things and becoming a scaremonger. It is rather in being well-informed in military strategy, in forever pondering one's resources of pacifying disturbances, in training one's soldiers without remiss, in rewarding those who have done meritorious deeds and punishing those who have committed crimes, in being correct in one's evaluation of bravery and cowardice, and in not forgetting this matter of "the battle" even when the world is at peace. It is simply brashness to make a specialty of the martial arts and to be absorbed in one's individual efforts. Such is certainly not the Way of the Warrior of a provincial lord or military commander.

There is no special technique in the military strategy of our clan. Its essentials are simply in carrying out the orders of the master and chief retainers carefully, and in the unity of our soldiers. The strength of our soldiers will be as hard as metal or stone if, during uneventful ordinary times, one will be sympathetic toward his retainers, give rewards without regret to those who deserve them, and demonstrate this attitude to all men, thus harmonizing by one's own sympathy the hearts of the upper and lower ranks and earnestly encouraging the bravery of one's soldiers. If such is done, there should be no doubt of victory.

Moreover, if a man who is a military commander has no sense of authority,[1] it will be difficult to command the masses. Yet, to understand this incorrectly, and purposely develop a sense of authority will cause great harm. When one understands "authority" to mean taking an attitude of intimidation toward everyone, acts in a high-blown manner even when meeting with the clan elders, uses rough words for matters of no consequence at all, refuses to listen to the admonitions of others, perseveres in his own mistakes, and forcibly shoves through his own opinions, even the clan elders will not rebuke him and he will likely be pulled along (a destructive path) by his own actions. If one acts like this even toward the clan elders alone, it will eventually reach to all his warriors, and by simply fearing the master they will have no thoughts of loyalty, will think only of their own positions, and will commit no true acts of service. Thus, if the master slights men because of his own pride, his retainers and even the common people will move away from him. One should understand well that this will inevitably bring on the destruction of his domain. What may be called true authority is brought about first in bearing oneself with the correct etiquette and in making clear the distinction between right and wrong, reward and punishment. If one will act in this way, and be neither prideful nor intimidating toward others, the retainers and common people will not respect him simply out of fear, or despise or make light of him, and he will be endowed with a natural authority.

It is essential that the above precepts are kept, and that the reserve funds for the castle are added to without remiss, bit by bit over the years. After a number of years this should amount to a great bit of wealth, and after 100 years our clan should be able to accumulate the better part of the currency in the realm.

Again, the present peaceful administration of the country is liable not to last forever. With the passage of 100, 150 or 200 years, there may well be some upheaval. There are examples of this in the past, and it is of utmost importance to be resolved in having a determined plan for this beforehand. When the country has been thrown into confusion and one's resources are few, it will be difficult to conduct military affairs and render meritorious services. And, it will be difficult to give ample protection to the fief.

You who are my descendants should tread in my footsteps, absolutely abide by these precepts, strive to be economical, behave yourselves all the more prudently, dispense benevolence to the people, be just in government, and carry on the family customs in a manly way. If you will do this, the entire country will hear of the benevolence of our clan and there will be many who are swayed to follow us. Particularly, there are samurai who understand the double Way of the scholar and warrior well, and who mean to make a name for themselves in this world. As such men choose their own masters well, they will without a doubt gather here even without being invited. This coming to pass, our clan will naturally excel others, and will clearly prosper both materially and in terms of authority.

However, to oppress the people and covet the possessions of the samurai in one's desire to become quickly prosperous is absolutely laying the foundation for the destruction of the fief.

Precious metals and jewels are not necessarily treasures. Rather, one should consider his samurai and the common people as his wealth, and bring them up with gentleness and benevolence. Gold and silver are not necessarily to be recklessly accumulated; and when one receives wealth and distinction naturally through years of meritorious deeds, no disasters are likely to follow.

Both lord and vassals should observe these principles well, manage things in a way that there will be no mistakes, and not act contrary to my precepts.

Again, there may be some among my descendants who act unjustly and selfishly, do not listen to admonitions, act freely without observing these precepts, and recklessly make expenditures. If this should occur, the clan elders should confer together and remove that man, choosing another with good character from my descendants to be lord. Thus will our house continue.

It is essential that the clan elders understand the purport of these things well, and pass them on to each and every one of my descendants.

It is vital that these articles be strictly and permanently observed.

To my son, Tadayuki
and the Chief Elders
Nagamasa

Notes

[1] 威 : This character is difficult to capture in a single English word. It carries the meaning of both dignity and authority and perhaps comes close to an ideal of dignified charisma. Needless to say, it was considered an essential during the Warring States Period.

BIBLIOGRAPHY
Textual Sources

Gunsho Ruiju, Vol. 15. Tokyo: Keizai Zasshisha, 1895.

Kamiko, Tadashi. *Busho Goroku*. Tokyo: Hyakusen Shobo, 1970.

Koyama, Keiichi. *Imagawa Ryoshun*. Tokyo: Sanseido, 1945.

Kurihara, Arano. *Koshu Hagakure*. Kumamoto: Seichosha, 1975.

Shinko Gunsho Ruiju, Vols. 17, 21. Tokyo: Naigai Shoseki Kabushiki Kaisha, 1931.

Yutaka, Takeru et alia, gen. ed. *Sengoku Shiryo Sosho*. Tokyo: Jinbutsu Oraisha, 1966. Vols. 3, 4, 5, *Koyogunkan*.

Yoshida, Yutaka. *Buke no Kakun*. Tokyo: Tokuma Shoten, 1973.

Zoku Gunsho Ruiju, Vol. 21. Tokyo: Zoku Gunsho Ruiju Kanseisha, 1924.

Zokuzoku Gunsho Ruiju, Vol. 10. Tokyo: Naigai Insatsu Kabushiki Kaisha, 1908.

Background Sources

Anesaki, M. *A History of Japanese Religion*. London: The Japanese Council, Institute of Pacific Relations, 1930.

Butler, Kenneth Dean. "The Heike Monogatari and the Japanese Warrior Ethic," *Harvard Journal of Asiatic Studies*, Vol. 29. Cambridge: Harvard-Yenching Institute, 1969.

Fairbank, John, Edwin Reischauer and Albert Craig. *East Asia: Tradition and Transformation*. Boston: Houghton Mifflin Company, 1973.

Giles, Lionel. *Sun Tzu on the Art of War*. Taipei: Literature House Ltd., 1964.

Griffith, Samuel. *Sun Tzu: The Art of War*. Oxford: Oxford University Press, 1971.

Hyakunensha, ed. *Rekishi Dokuhon* (special edition). "Sengoku no Busho Nihyaku-nana Ketsu," Summer, 1977. Vol. 3.

Iwanami Bunko, 884-885a. Tokyo: Iwanami Shoten, 1973. Kanaya, Osamu, ed. *Rongo*.

Kitagawa, H., and B. Tsuchida. Trans. *The Tale of Heike*. Tokyo: University of Tokyo Press, 1975.

Lu, David. *Sources of Japanese History*, Vol. 1. New York: McGraw-Hill, 1974.

McCullough, Helen. *The Taiheiki: A Chronicle of Medieval Japan.* New York: Columbia University Press, 1959.

Meikai Koten Gakushu Shirizu, 20 Vols. Tokyo: Sanseido, 1973. *Konjaku Monogatari, Uji Shui Monogatari.*

Morris, Ivan. *The World of the Shining Prince: Court Life in Ancient Japan.* Harmondsworth: Penguin, 1969.

Murasaki, Shikibu. *The Tale of Genji.* Translated by Arthur Waley. New York: The Literary Guild, 1935.

Naramoto, Tatsuya. *Bushido no Keifu.* Tokyo: Chuo Koronsha, 1971.

Nihon Rekishi Bunko, Vol. 9. Tokyo: Kodansha, 1975. *Sengoku no Busho,* by Sasaki, Ginya.

Nihon Shiso Taikei, Vol. 32. Tokyo: Iwanami Shoten, 1970. *Yamaga Soko.*

Philippi, Donald. Trans. *Kojiki.* Tokyo: University of Tokyo Press, 1968.

Sagara, Toru, ed. *Nihon no Shiso,* 20 Vols. Tokyo: Chikuma Shobo, 1969. Vol. 9, *Koyogunkan, Gorinsho, Hagakure Shu.*

Sansom, George. *A History of Japan to 1334.* Stanford: Stanford Unversity Press, 1958.

Sansom, George. *A History of Japan, 1334-1615.* Stanford: Stanford University Press, 1961.

Shintei Chugoku Koten Sen, 20 Vols. Tokyo: Asahi Shinbunsha, 1967. Vol. 4, *Daigaku, Chuyo,* by Shimada Kenji.

Yamamoto, Tsunetomo. *Hagakure.* Translated by William Wilson. Tokyo: Kodansha, 1979.

Varley, Paul. *The Onin War.* New York: Columbia University Press, 1967.

Dictionaries

Dai Kan-wa Jiten, 12 Vols. Morohashi, Tetsuji, comp. Tokyo: Daishokan Shoten, 1960.

Kadokawa Kan-wa Chujiten. Kaizuka, Shigeki, Iwatomo Fujino and Shinobu Ono, eds. Tokyo: Kadokawa Shoten, 1974.

Nihon Kokugo Daijiten, 20 Vols. Nihon Daijiten Kanko Kai, ed. Tokyo: Shogakkan, 1977.